Your Soul Explained

Don Durrett

ISBN: 979-8-8689-5686-7

www.dondurrett.com

Books by Don Durrett

Stranger From The Past

Finding Your Soul

Conversations With an Immortal

Spirit Club

Last of the Gnostics

The Gathering

Ascension Training

Team Creator

The Path Forward

Get Healthy / Stay Healthy

America's Political Cold War

Post America: A New Constitution

The Demise of America

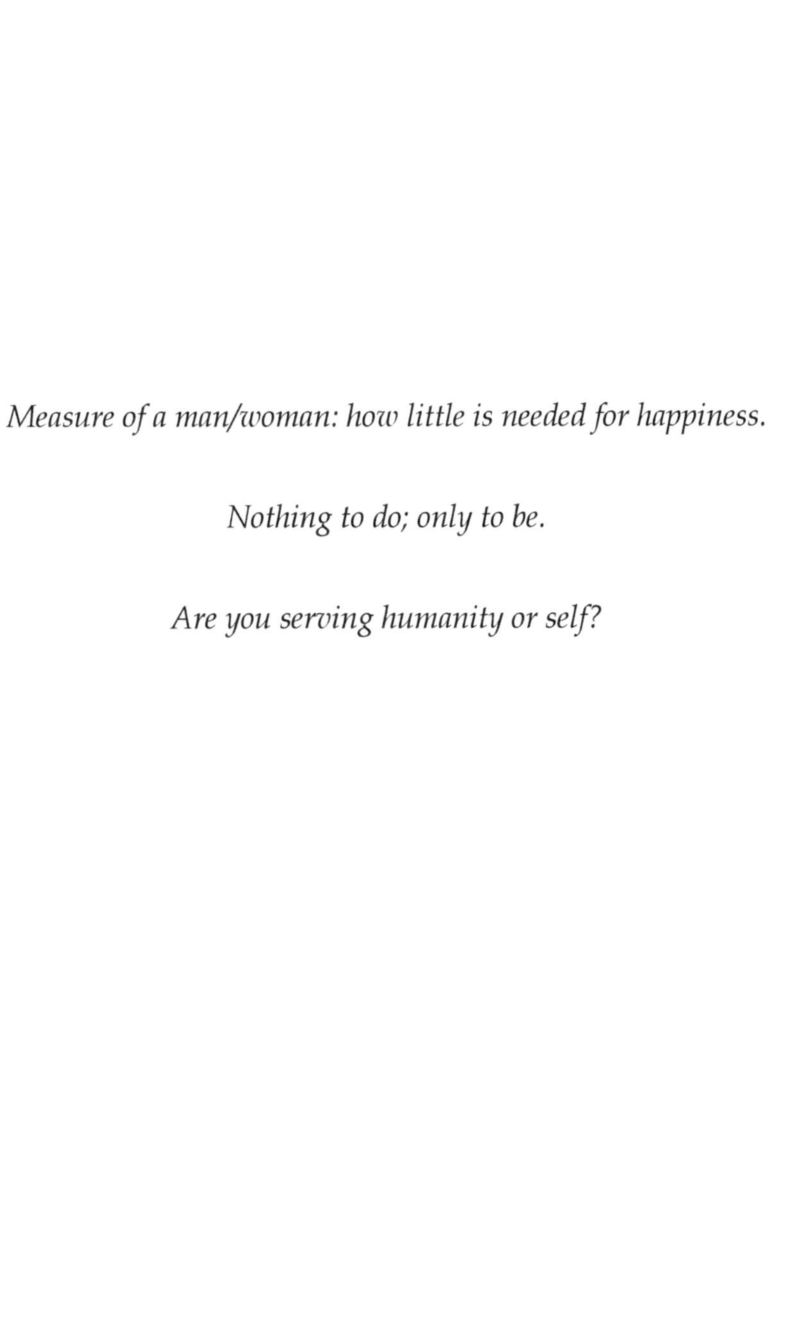

Measure of a man/woman: how little is needed for happiness.

Nothing to do; only to be.

Are you serving humanity or self?

CONTENTS

INTRODUCTION

We are on the precipice of a New Age, or if you prefer, New Era or New Civilization. Soon, the United States and the rest of the world will begin to change dramatically. Within a generation, society will have changed so radically that we will not recognize it. The reason for this transformation is that our beliefs are going to change. That may sound like hyperbole, but many of our current beliefs have become obsolete, with many of them based on fallacies (I will be writing about these fallacies in this book).

As a society, we are going to change our most fundamental credos. We will do so mostly because our beliefs will change, but also in order to create a more humane civilization. Soon, new foundations and societal structures will begin to take hold that will reshape society. This won't happen until society breaks down, which has probably already begun since I wrote this book.

The United States will not be united for much longer. In fact, its near-term destiny is to break up into a series of countries. This is now unavoidable and the only outcome. The only question is how these new countries are reshaped based on the new unfolding beliefs.

The metamorphosis that will occur over the next generation is of a magnitude that is difficult to imagine. Civilization will literally transform. This will not be a subtle shift, but rather a dramatic and chaotic experience for which most people are unprepared.

Everything from our economic system to our political system will be completely transformed. When this reformation is complete, a new civilization will arise, one very different from today's. You may already be aware of the forces reshaping society, perhaps even anticipating a global upheaval. This book provides insight into the coming changes and will help you understand what lies ahead.

Few people are aware of the dramatic alterations that are upon us. Now, in the new millennium, many people see society as unstable and in dire need of reformulation. This book and others like it will be the basis for the new model. As incredible as it sounds, we are the generation that will determine the foundation for the next civilization.

What is coming is not expected. This change to humanity is mostly going to be a spiritual shift, which very few are expecting. In fact, our beliefs are going to rapidly change over the next few decades. The rapidity of change will be quite shocking to most. Many will try to hold on to their old beliefs, but as you read this book, you will see that won't work for them. They will be like fish swimming against the current.

* * * * *

I use the terms New Age, New Ager, Lightworker, and New Age Movement in my writing. These terms have been given various definitions and used in different contexts. I use them for one purpose: to point out that there is a group of people who believe that we are on the verge of a spiritual transformation. This New Age group – for the most part – holds the following beliefs:

- We are God, and so is everyone and everything else.
- There is only one consciousness, which we all share.
- There is no separation between anything, because everything is consciously interrelated.
- Everyone's life is perfect and was planned in advance.
- Everyone creates their own reality by their beliefs, thoughts, and intent.

- There are no accidents and no victims.
- Life on this planet is an illusion, and only the soul is real.
- Reincarnation is a reality, and this is no one's first lifetime.
- Spirituality is a personal matter and a long journey.

Whereas this group opposes being labeled as New Agers and argues that a New Age movement does not even exist, their affinity with this list of core beliefs does place them in a unique position. This is the group of people who are ushering in this New Age. Their beliefs and intent, along with their actions and behaviors, are the reason for this transformation. Without them, it would not be happening.

Last, I do not have all the answers, and everyone holds their own personal truth. One book of spiritual material is just that: one book. There is not one book or one path that leads to enlightenment. We each have a different journey to take, and on that journey, we will each use different beliefs. My point is that the ideas expounded in this book are not the definitive truth. I may make claims of truth, but that just means it is my truth.

This is the deepest spiritual philosophy I have written since most of my metaphysical books are stories and don't lend themselves to an in-depth dive into spiritual ideas and concepts. I have mostly written stories because they are easier to read and an easier way to share metaphysical concepts.

If you have not read any of my spiritual books or New Age material, then many of the ideas in the book will be new to you, or, at the very least, contrary to what you currently believe. For this reason, I recommend that you first read one of my previous spiritual books. That way, this book will be more enjoyable to read. It's probably better to do a warmup than just dive right in. I say that because this material is dense. Be prepared to get your brain overloaded.

Note: Some of you may be confused by my usage of em dashes and parentheses, which I use a lot in this book. I use em dashes for information that is needed to remove confusion. I use parentheses for added information that is optional but can add clarity.

Note: At the very end of my suggested reading list, there are two YouTube channels. I highly recommend that you watch these if you enjoy this book. They are loaded with good information.

* * * * *

I think this might be my last spiritual book. I turned 63 this year, which is a 9, and could be completion. Also, I don't think I have much more to say that hasn't already been said in my previous books. For this reason, I'm going to include a bit of my personal history and some personal information.

First off, I want to say that I think that this book, along with my other spiritual books, is immensely powerful information. I'm stunned that nobody else feels that way. I hope that changes in the future.

I generally get called by my spirit guides to write my next book. Usually, the title comes to me, or sometimes the outline of the plot. This one came to me in August 2023. It came in loud and clear as the title of the book. I was also told to review and edit all of my previous spiritual books before I began. I wasn't excited about that ordeal and the hard work that would be required. But I have learned not to argue with my spirit guides. I have come to learn that they know what is best.

I've always known that my book writing is leading to something. I don't know what, but there is an end game at some point. Perhaps this book is that endpoint since they asked me to clean up all of the others in advance. That ordeal was actually invigorating, although it took a lot of hard work. I was able to add significant information to each one. They are now improved from a fresh edit, and many of them substantially so.

This book will replace both New Thinking for the New Age and The Way (if you have a copy of those, they are rare, with less than 25 copies of each printed), which were my only other non-story spiritual philosophy books. This will leave me with eight spiritual books that are stories (see list below), along with this book on spiritual philosophy, and finally, The Path Forward, which is my vision of the coming future. Ironically, I named my company Ten Books Publishing, which is my book count for spiritual books. A coincidence?

- A Stranger From The Past
- Finding Your Soul
- Conversations With an Immortal
- Spirit Club
- Last of the Gnostics
- Ascension Training
- The Gathering
- Team Creator

I'm an odd, introverted duck. I've had a difficult time in personal relationships and have lost many close friends. They tend to get tired of my oddness and fall away. An astrologer read my natal horoscope in 1991 and told me that she didn't understand what I was doing in America. She said that nobody cared for what I had to say and that I should be in a monastery or an ashram in India.

She was spot on. The only person who I am sure loved me in this lifetime was my mother, who was an angel. The rest of my family wasn't quite sure who I was. My dad never liked me that much, and we had a strained relationship from my childhood onward. When my mother passed in 2005, life got more difficult. I felt like I was alone in the world. To make matters worse, close friends kept falling away. I hope some of them come back, but it's not looking great.

The reason for my relationship issues is that I've been on a spirit quest my entire life. I know that now. And my spirit quest is the ultimate one: I want to know the truth of who I am, the truth of reality, and the truth of God. Everything else is just noise.

To make matters worse, I refuse to believe that utopia isn't possible. My idealism is so extreme that I reject any pretense of settling for something less than a perfect society.

When you combine those two driving forces, I have been on an endless quest to achieve the unobtainable. But the universe did this on purpose so that I would write these books. I know that now.

I've had a terrible time finding a romantic partner. I've had at least three chances to get married but passed on all of them because it didn't feel right. I'm a restless 5 of diamonds who demands his freedom. I know what a good match will be, and the universe has refused to provide it. And I think I know why: the universe wanted these books written. Now, I'm at the stage of life where the odds aren't great that I will find her. Maybe, maybe not. I still have hope. I know what I need, and she hasn't shown up yet.

I know why I'm on this planet. I came to write these books and help a few souls find the truth. So far, that has not been rewarding, but I have to believe my work was not in vain.

I feel a lot of empathy for those who have a hard life and feel alone. It's not an easy road. I don't like living alone, but the universe, or my higher self, thought it was best for this lifetime. I'm hoping my journey gets easier as I enter my retirement years. They say people get happier as they get older.

My plan is to find a way to help others find their spiritual truth through ways other than writing additional books. This could be from blogging, podcasts, or public speaking. We'll see what unfolds.

Don Durrett

October 2023

CHAPTER ONE

Who Are We? Why Are We Here?

Who are we? We are God. I know that may sound overwhelming, but it's true. This is not subjective truth. It's objective truth. Although I know it's true, you will have to find out for yourself, and science won't definitively prove it until around 2050.

The truth is that there is only one consciousness which we all share. This is why a mother can know if her child was in an accident and suddenly become frantic. Or, why telepathy is possible.

Separation is a lie. There is no separation between us and God. In fact, there is no separation between us and anything. Our consciousness is part of God's consciousness, and God's consciousness makes up the *whole*. This fact makes us eternal, perfect, and divine.

You may think that's an interesting theory, but not only is it the truth, but that truth will soon be released to humanity. Not only will it be released, but it will become the foundation for the next civilization, which our generation will be the progenitors.

Since I'm dropping truth bombs, I might as well tell you the meaning of life, which is to expand our awareness, which we do through experience. In other words, the reason we are here is to *experience*. So, this planet is a school where we have come to learn.

Wait a minute, Don. If what you are saying is true, then how come I haven't heard about these ideas? All this sounds preposterous. My response to that is that the truth is always true. The world is based on lies, and now the truth is coming out. It could not come out until humanity was ready, but that time is quickly approaching.

As our spiritual awareness increases, we become aware of God. This awareness is not through faith or belief, but through knowing. We come to *know* God. Slowly, through many incarnations, we become enlightened, and consciously aware that we are God. Our individuality is an illusion. Under the façade of our ego-personality is a powerful soul that is essentially one with God. Duality is an illusion. All that exists is oneness.

God is All That Is. Nothing that exists is separate from God. Everything is connected through an interrelated web of consciousness. God is not a being, but is consciousness itself, an integrated consciousness. This is possible because everything that exists was created by God *from* God. In other words, God can create only from itself. We are a piece of God that was spawned from the essence of God, as were all things. When an essence is spawned, it remains part of the whole, part of God's consciousness. This is where our consciousness comes from, which can also be described as the source of life. And because we are connected to the source, we have an instinctive desire for spirituality and to remember our heritage. In fact, it is inevitable that we find our way back home, although perhaps not in this lifetime. This is why enlightenment is a long journey.

So, now you know why we exist. We are the means for God to experience life.

* * * * *

Life on the physical plane – on a planet such as Earth – allows God to experience the infinite. God is interested in *all* experiences. One experience may be negative, another positive, but both are of God. Thus, all experiences are valid. There is no right or wrong, no good or bad. God does not judge or place value judgments on experience. Judgment is not possible because God is All That Is … and God does not judge itself.

Experiences can have a *positive* or *negative* outcome. This is where free will comes in. We get to choose our experiences. We can choose to learn using positive *or* negative. But we don't get a free pass when we choose to learn through negative experiences. Thus, the consequences of our choices are quite real. The consequences, or effects, are called *karma*, which is an imbalance of energy that must be re-balanced. Most of us add karma with our negative actions, then redress the imbalance with positive actions. Some souls become so out of balance that they regress spiritually, although this is rare.

There is not a saint among us. We all choose to have negative experiences with our free will. That is how we learn. Maybe we have been mostly good in this life, but that is not the case in every life. We all have dirty laundry and past deeds that we regret. Someone who appears to be a saint in this lifetime was a scoundrel in another lifetime.

We are in school. In fact, on the higher etheric planes of existence, Earth is called a school. Moreover, Earth is considered a very challenging school, one of the most challenging in the universe. Souls who have incarnated on

Earth are highly respected on the etheric spiritual planes. You have to be courageous to come here, especially during this era. My soul group didn't want to come, and I incarnated by myself. I didn't want to miss this opportunity. Neither did you.

The reason it is so challenging on Earth is because we experience limitation in an environment with a high level of negative energy. Our awareness of God – our true self – is severely limited. This provides an ideal environment in which to learn, although also one where it is easy to go astray. If it were not for the limitations, we would not be able to experience such a wide array of possibilities. The duality of good and bad – positive and negative – could not exist without these limitations.

There is a saying that the greatest trick Satan plays is to convince us that he does not exist. Well, God has played a larger trick. God gave us amnesia so that we would not remember we are *one*. This is how God created duality, because once we realize who we are, the illusion is shattered, and duality loses its hold. *That* is what is about to happen to our generation.

Where we come from is not the physical universe, or what can be called the *physical plane*. The physical plane is an illusion and is not real. It is made up of only one substance, energy, which is vibrating at a certain frequency. Nothing on the physical plane is solid. For instance, our bodies vibrate at around 80,000 to 100,000 cycles per second (the more evolved you are, the higher you vibrate). This is why people can disappear (if you think this is impossible, study the Yogis in India).

The physical plane is a place, as previously mentioned, that was created by God (with our help) to experience the infinite and for the expansion of our spiritual awareness.

When we incarnate, we leave home, which is the etheric spiritual plane, and venture on a journey into the physical plane. We do this with one goal in mind: to expand our spiritual awareness. As we become more aware of our oneness with God, our God-like creative abilities increase. We literally become God-like over a long period of time and a multitude of experiences.

* * * * *

We are not physical. We are spirit. Our physical body is used to house our soul during this journey. The body is temporary, whereas the soul is immortal and indestructible. In fact, the soul is what can be called pure energy. It is literally the essence of God. On the other hand, our body is nothing more than a costume. From the soul's perspective, the body is analogous to a piece of clothing, something to wear for a short period of time.

Our true self – our soul – is much more than is generally perceived. It is this lack of awareness that creates our experiences. Thus, the more limited our awareness, the more likely we are to have negative experiences. Conversely, as humanity becomes more spiritually aware, negativity will begin to diminish.

Life is about becoming more spiritually aware, or in other words, it is about remembering who we are. Thus, in many respects, our journey is a series of aha! moments of remembering. For this reason, there is nothing to achieve, only to become more conscious. Moreover, as Buddha came to realize, there is nothing to *do*. We are here to *experience*, and that is all. Through experience, we naturally expand our consciousness. An effort to become more spiritually aware is not even required. It is a natural process. Yes, we can speed up the process with effort, but just living is enough to grow spiritually. We are all growing, except the rare soul who takes the road of negativity to the extreme, lifetime after lifetime.

Am I saying life is meaningless? Quite the contrary. I'm saying meaning is the byproduct of experience. Thus, any experience, both positive or negative, ignites spiritual growth and expansion of consciousness. Life itself is the meaning. It does not matter what experiences we have; we still grow. This is why this lifetime is so precious and such a gift.

Today, Western civilization focuses on achievement. Moreover, we view non-technological cultures, such as the Native Americans or Aborigines, as primitive. Is one culture better than another? Is one life lived in one culture more conducive to enlightenment than another? No. *Every* experience leads to the expansion of consciousness.

Each culture provides an array of experiences. Souls who are looking for particular experiences incarnate into those cultures. One culture is not better than another. Each provides unique situations that match what a soul needs.

We are God, and we are on Earth to experience a life that fits with what our soul needs. From this experience, our consciousness expands. For most of us, the expansion is very slight, or what I like to call a *blip* of growth. However, it is one more step toward our enlightenment. A few souls will have an epiphany and make great strides toward enlightenment in this lifetime. That could be you.

I do know this: the experiences we choose in this lifetime carry over to the spiritual plane and into our future lives. Thus, our experiences have ramifications. We do not get to clear the slate once we arrive in heaven. This life counts more than we know. All of the karma that we accumulate must be accounted for. As the saying goes, we can do this the easy way, or the hard way. Either way, the outcome is the same: enlightenment.

CHAPTER TWO

Beliefs

Beliefs are the most important facet of our lives because they create our experiences. Our intent and thoughts are just as important, but those stem from our beliefs. So, it all begins with our beliefs.

How significant are beliefs? Well, if we each create our lives through our beliefs, then what could be more significant? *Everything* that happens in our lives is from the manifestation of a belief.

Life does not happen to us. We *create* it. Not one thing happens in life that is not the result of our beliefs. Everything, from an accident to the people we attract into our lives, occurs from our thoughts. Given this importance, you would think we would be concerned about what we believe. On the contrary, most people take their beliefs for granted and rarely analyze them to see how they are impacting their lives. For instance, have you ever journaled your thoughts? Most people have not.

I was surprised at how much my life changed once I began writing down what I believed. I had to ponder how my beliefs impacted my life. For instance, the simple idea of who deserves forgiveness opened a pandora's box of ramifications. I finally (after a few years!) came to the conclusion that everyone deserves forgiveness, especially ourselves. Amazingly, the average person refuses to forgive themselves, let alone others. This belief is a trap, and most people have no idea that they are trapped. What are they trapped from? Recognizing the oneness in the world, and thus learning how to love themselves and others unconditionally.

Let me try to explain how life really works. Each of us is vibrating at a certain rate, a certain frequency. This vibration – faster is better – reflects our level of spiritual awareness, our current beliefs, and our past lives. From this combination, our life unfolds. Our frequency, which impacts our beliefs, attracts our experiences. Our horoscope, family, and culture also play important roles, but it is our frequency and beliefs that put everything into motion. And note that our beliefs can speed up our frequency. Thus, if you change your beliefs, you change your life. You may not realize it, but this book could change your life. Any book could, but this one is all about beliefs.

One amazing thing I have noticed over the years is how few people can read my books. What is the problem? Simply this: my books require you to question your beliefs. People hate to do that. They would prefer to keep their beliefs on autopilot, and never question them.

Our beliefs determine the extent to which we feel emotions such as fear, anxiety, and love. Thus, we *create* these emotions. Everyone is a creator, creating his or her own life through his or her beliefs. Conversely, if we change our beliefs, we change our lives.

Most people do not realize that their convictions are creating their reality. Conversely, they do not believe they can alter their lives or that they are in charge of their lives. Even as you are reading this, you probably do not believe me. You probably believe that life is happening *to* you. However, if you transform that belief, you can remodel your life.

Many people presume that everything is happening by chance, but that is the furthest thing from the truth. Our beliefs create a frequency, and this frequency attracts accordingly. Remember, we are vibrating energy. Our bodies are not solid, and our soul is pure energy (it's not made from molecules, atoms, and electrons), which overlays our body. One of the laws of the universe is that *like attracts like*. We cannot have any experience that does not match our frequency. It is impossible.

For instance, if you walk into a room of one hundred people, and there is someone in the room with a similar frequency as yours, you will probably notice that person. You might not talk with him or her, but you easily could if the opportunity presented itself. Life, in many respects, is like that room of people. We attract and are attracted. We are like magnets, inviting events into our lives. And it is our beliefs, frequency, horoscope, and level of spiritual awareness that affect the magnet.

The ideas presented in this book are generally only understood by old souls. However, this knowledge is becoming more widespread as the energy vibration (frequency) of the planet increases. In the 1980s, if you told people their beliefs created every event in their lives, they questioned your sanity. Now, in the new millennium, many people accept this concept and incorporate it into their lives.

When I had my natal horoscope done in 1990 by a professional astrologer, she told me three things that were uncannily accurate. First, she didn't know why I was in this country because my beliefs were so incongruent with this culture. She said nobody cared about what I had to say and that I belonged in a monastery in India. Second, she said I would likely remain single. Third, my ability to grasp spiritual knowledge was unlimited.

When I gave my parents my first book, my dad recommended that I commit suicide (he was serious). My mom said to never ask her to read another of my books. As you can see, the astrologer was spot on! Alas, the changes to

our beliefs will be so profound that it takes someone like me
– an outsider – to expose the truth.

* * * * *

Beliefs are personal and are based on personal experience.
Thus, beliefs divide people who have had different
experiences. This is why there is so much antagonism and
conflict in the world. This is why America has split into
a series of interest groups. Beliefs literally create conflict.
This is why all religions are in their final days. Group-based
spirituality – religion – will soon be replaced with individual-
based spirituality.

Beliefs must be *personal*. Moreover, no two people
can have the same understanding of God, nor do any two
people have the same beliefs. Everyone has his or her own,
unique beliefs. For this reason, beliefs have no place in the
organization of society. We must base society on what we
know, not on what we believe.

The positive traits of humanity – peace, love, freedom,
equality, caring, compassion, friendship, family, integrity –
are not beliefs, but can easily be the basis for the organization
of society. We can create a secular society where spirituality
is individual-based and without religion. Spirituality can be
a personal matter, with spiritual beliefs having nothing to
do with the organization of society. We can create a society
based on what we *know*.

I expect to witness the birth of this new society, and I
believe this will occur as we come to recognize the fallacy
of our current beliefs, such as the following: we are separate
from God and from each other; this is our first lifetime;
capitalism in its current form is good; equality and fairness
exist; individual sovereignty is not important; a large
government is not a problem. Once enough people realize

that many of our beliefs are a fallacy, society will change. This critical mass point is not that far away.

Besides the fact that religious beliefs create conflict, there is an even better reason to drop our group beliefs: they clog the mind and prevent us from knowing the *truth*. Truth is found in the present moment, with an uncluttered mind. We cannot find the truth from the past, only *now*. Focusing on religious dogma as a group will not help us find the truth.

All the great spiritual teachers have told us to know ourselves. Dropping our group beliefs is the beginning of knowing the truth. Once we focus on humanity's needs from a clear vantage point, instead of being hindered by group beliefs based on the past, we can create a better world.

* * * * *

Beliefs can easily prevent freedom. Freedom is an idea. Freedom is not something given to us. It is something that is taken. It is an *awareness* that we are free. It is not something that is created through laws. For instance, following a system, such as the United States Constitution and Bill of Rights, will never provide true freedom. Anything written into law are privileges that can be revoked. Believing that a system of laws can provide freedom only creates a barrier to freedom. True freedom is the freedom to discover each moment anew, without any rules hindering that discovery.

Once you understand that beliefs can prevent freedom, you can create a society that cherishes freedom and makes sure that it isn't hindered just because someone believes that it should be. Is this a utopian idea? Sure, but that is where society is headed once it accepts the belief that we are all one.

Beliefs have many negative effects (in addition to restricting freedom), yet we are tethered to them. Beliefs isolate us from each other; they create conditions for war; they hide us from the truth; they prevent us from knowing ourselves; and they hold us back from creating a utopian world.

You may be wondering how we can drop our group beliefs and begin to rely on truth. First, we have to change ourselves before we can change society. We have to change our personal beliefs, one person at a time. This change is already occurring as more and more people expose themselves to metaphysics. It is inevitable that millions of people will change their spiritual beliefs and expand their definitions of God and what it means to be human. That change is occurring today and is quickly reaching critical mass, where the impact will transform society. In many respects, humanity is on a spiritual quest to find the truth, one person at a time.

* * * * *

Let's look at some of these new beliefs. The first and most important one is that there is only one consciousness that we all share. This new belief can only be kept secret for a few more years because it is time for this truth to be revealed. From this new belief, we will see many others spawned.

Another important one is the frequency of love. Many will learn how to be a frequency of love by using their belief in oneness. You do this by remaining neutral and accepting everything that happens in your life as either a blessing or an opportunity. By being neutral, that means you don't react in a stressful manner to events in your life. Instead, you maintain unconditional love with an awareness that we are all interrelated.

People will learn that the more you love yourself, the more it will be reflected back to you. Why? Because your beliefs create your reality, and unity begins with self-love. That's the starting point.

Conversely, negative thoughts and a lack of self-love are detrimental. Why is this? Because we are the divine, and the divine only knows unlimitedness, joy, success, positive feelings, optimism, perfection, and omnipotence. These beliefs are our natural state and where we find harmony in our lives. So, when you limit yourself, the divine limits your experiences. This is another way of saying that we pull ourselves down with negative thoughts and beliefs.

Fear is only a belief. Fear and the truth cannot coexist. Why is this? Because the divine cannot know fear, and we are the divine. So, when we experience fear, we are creating an illusion. We can hold the belief, "What if something bad happens?" or "What if something good happens?" both are beliefs. You can hold either one. The universe will give you the one you ask for. So, choose wisely!

All of our personal problems manifest from the denial of the divine. In fact, denial of the divine is the only blasphemy. Those two sentences you should write down and read for the next 30 days! Why? Because they are the key to your happiness and peace of mind. Once you see that all is divine, your life will begin to work. Normally, making this type of drastic change to your beliefs would not be necessary. However, what is about to transpire on this planet does make it necessary. Or else you will be swimming against the current, pretending that the old beliefs are valid.

Here's a good one. It's called co-resonance. This is when you judge someone else as lacking, and you actually pull yourself down! Who knew? You don't even know that you are doing this to yourself. It's another trap. The divine knows that we are all one, so when you invoke separation by judging another as less than perfect, the divine immediately recognizes that we lack the truth and *decreases* our frequency! Since we lack the truth, the universe limits us. Ouch.

Here's the good news! Co-resonance works in the opposite manner. When we don't judge others, the divine recognizes that we do know the truth and *increases* our frequency! Remember when I said that our beliefs can change our frequency? Ladies and gentlemen, I give you co-resonance. Use it wisely. Hint: When you bless another, you bless yourself. When you love another, you love yourself. When you damn another, you damn yourself.

Desire – temptation – is the destroyer. Disinterest is the redeemer. I will be talking more about this later on when I discuss ego. The point I want to make here is that the belief in having fun as the meaning of life can destroy your spirituality. Temptations can lead you down a dark path. If you want to align with your higher self and be spirit-led, then hedonism has to be reigned in, or else it will lead you astray.

Two final points for this chapter on beliefs. First, make the present moment your friend. Recognize that life only gives you blessings or opportunities and that everything else is an illusion. Expect good things and create good things. Second, recognize that fear lowers your vibration/frequency. Always remain positive about your life and in the present moment. Don't allow fear in. Kick it out of your life and keep it out. This can only be done through beliefs. So, work on them!

CHAPTER THREE

Christianity is Based on Fallacy

One time a Christian asked me who I thought God was. I replied, "Me and you." You should have seen his eyes. He thought he was talking to Satan. All he could say was, "The occult is very dangerous. You should be careful with what you read."

In 1989, I read a book that changed my life. In that book, Nostradamus stated that Christianity would not last much longer and that Christianity was in its "sunset." He further stated that the New Age movement would be the basis for what would replace Christianity. At that time, I was a Christian who believed that the Bible was essentially correct. Today, I identify with the New Age movement and believe the Bible is essentially false – not the story of Jesus, but the beliefs it espouses.

Christianity is based on three major beliefs. The first is the duality of right and wrong – good and evil. The second is the belief that God is separate from us. The third is that Jesus is the son of God. I do not deny this last belief, but you and I are also sons and daughters of God. The first two beliefs will be revealed to be false and will be replaced by beliefs held by the New Age movement.

The beliefs in right and wrong (explained in more detail later), as well as the belief in separation, will be replaced by the concept of oneness. People will recognize that we are all interconnected and, in essence, *one*. I do not deny that good and evil both exist. I do deny that one is right and the other is wrong, or that one is God and the other is Satan, or that someone can always identify evil. From a metaphysical standpoint, there is no such thing as right and wrong, because God is *all*, and God is perfect. In other words, God is Satan, and God is us. God was Hitler, as well as Mother Teresa.

Christianity took the belief in the duality of good and evil and concluded that good is right and evil is wrong. The outcome was our Western civilization, which is collapsing because of this fallacy. Many want to blame the degradation on Satan, but it is our false beliefs that are the culprit.

Look at the result of the belief in duality. Today everyone lives under a microscope, constantly being judged by other people. We cannot so much as live our lives without other people questioning our choices. Everyone is expected to conform and do the right thing. Those who conform and do the right thing are the good guys. Those who do not are the bad guys. We are all given labels to determine where we reside along the continuum of good versus evil.

In essence, the belief in duality has created a judgmental civilization. No one is allowed to do what they want unless it is sanctioned by society. Thus, everything is conditional based on what is accepted as proper (i.e., good). There is so much judgment going on that our souls are blocked from finding the truth.

Not only is society judgmental, but it is also not free. The ultimate freedom is to be able to do what we want without judgment. Moreover, freedom and unconditional love go hand in hand. Now you know why unconditional love is so rare today. If we truly love someone unconditionally, we allow them the freedom to live as they want. Remember Sting's song, "If you love somebody, set them free...."?

Today, love is conditional because of our judgmental civilization. People are loved according to their ability to adhere to what is accepted. Those who fit in are loved. Those who go against the grain are deprived of love. The concept of equality has no meaning. We love our heroes and denigrate our criminals. We do not treat each other equally, not even close.

For the most part, we judge people because we believe God judges people. Christianity took the belief of duality and created a civilization that perceives that God loves by degree. The result has been a perception that those who are good deserve to be loved more than those who are bad. According to this belief, God is good, and God punishes those who are bad.

The second belief, that God is separate from us, is related to the belief in good and bad. If God is good and humankind is bad, then we must be separate from God. However, is this belief correct? No, it is not.

People today are prevented from loving strangers because the belief in separation is so strong. Children are taught not to talk to strangers. We are conditioned as kids that everyone is different and that strangers are not to be trusted. Our parents tell us to stay away from bad people. We are conditioned to think in terms of good and bad. For instance, drugs are bad, not doing homework is bad, getting in trouble is bad, not eating dinner is bad. The list is endless. Children are rewarded with love only for being good, such as getting good grades or making the all-star team.

The movie *Dead Poets Society* was a revealing depiction of how we condition our children. In this story about an elite prep school for high school boys, one student kills himself because his father will not allow him to make his own decisions. How many children have had to endure the tyranny of their parents and society?

The conditioning continues after high school. We are expected to get a job and are pressured into being productive members of society. Those who are productive are rewarded and respected, and those who are not are ridiculed.

Why is there so much pressure to be productive and achievement-oriented? The answer is from the belief in separation. We perceive ourselves to be individuals instead of interrelated. What else is there left to do but differentiate ourselves through achievement? In addition to our belief in separation, there are Biblical references to prospering. The Christian value "God wants us to prosper" is a strong determinant in Western culture.

The belief in separation is the reason we reward productive people and judge the nonproductive. This is also the reason the homeless problem has been largely ignored (it has through 2023). People do not feel an affinity with the homeless because they are not productive and thereby deserve the judgment of God.

Most people believe they are separate from God. From this perception came the belief that people are also separate from one another. The ramifications of this belief led to a civilization based on judgment.

Most people also believe that evil is separate from God. Thus, evil is something that infects humans, and then God judges them as unworthy. Moreover, most Christians believe that God will accept only people who reject evil. On one hand, we have good (God). On the other, we have evil (Satan). This is the basis for the current duality of right and wrong. I contend that this duality is a fallacy.

Politicians spend an inordinate amount of time making laws to fight evil. Anything they perceive as wrong is outlawed. Many believe that God needs our help to fight evil and that it is our duty. President Reagan called Russia the Evil Empire. President George W. Bush has called Iraq, Iran, and North Korea the Axis of Evil. Christians are the biggest supporters of the fight against evil. The Christian God is usually mentioned when the word *evil* is used in a speech by politicians. The main objective for involvement in politics by Christians is to fight evil. The morality of abortion has inflamed many Christians to wage a political struggle against it. Today, as I write this, a fundamentalist Christian killed two receptionists at abortion clinics in Massachusetts.

Did not Jesus say to love our enemies? How can we love our enemies if we kill them? I submit that Christianity in its present form, is nothing more than a political organization. Christians are waging a political fight against people whose beliefs are different from theirs.

Politics in America has turned into a religious battle. Christians are lined up against so-called evil. Abortion, homosexuals, single parents, drug users, criminals, illegal aliens, and welfare recipients are considered evil elements in society.

* * * * *

Most people in the New Age movement are aware that duality is an illusion, and that duality cannot exist because everything is *one*. Thus, evil is part of us all and a reflection of us all. Evil is a reflection of the state of consciousness of humanity. If someone decides to be evil, there must be a reason for it to manifest. Moreover, society must have created that reason. Thus, if we want to reduce evil in society, then we must change ourselves first and not blame so-called evil people.

Christians have a strong belief that God will judge everyone's behavior in terms of morality. Many Christians believe that if we live by the wrong values, we will be condemned to hell. This has led to a pervasive fear, which has created a subtle undertone for the entire Christian faith. In essence, Christians are afraid of God. They are afraid God will not judge them or their family members as worthy. Again, another fallacy. We are God. Thus, they are afraid of themselves.

As far as spirituality goes, Christianity is lacking. Currently, Christians do not recognize their divinity. Instead, they perceive themselves to be creations of a fickle God, one who has the power to grant either eternal life in heaven or to forsake them to hell. This has led to a religion based on fear and a preoccupation with morality, especially the morality of others.

Today, Christians are experts at discerning (judging) evil. Thus, instead of loving everyone, they point at everyone who is not living up to Christian ideals. This will be the reason for the demise of Christianity in its current form. Even Jesus gave them a proper warning: "Let he who is without sin cast the first stone...." The lesson is clear: tread lightly when you judge another.

Christians have been conditioned to believe that God does not like evil. The concept that God is evil is anathema to Christians. If you confront Christians with this idea, they become defensive and angry. Where does this anger come from? Fear. Christians are afraid of God. This might not be apparent on the surface, but Christian beliefs do instill a sense of fear. They are conditioned, by accepting church dogma, to believe that God is separate from us and that He is a fickle, judgmental God.

Many Christians believe that God loves them, but even they are compelled by fear … if not for themselves, then for their loved ones, families, and friends. Christians are anxious that God might not love their loved ones as much as them. Thus, a pervasive anxiety envelops Christians. Does God love my son or daughter?

The foundation of Christianity was based on the belief that God is separate from us. This is where the concept of judgment came from, as well as the belief that God is going to judge us. It is quite common to hear Christians proudly state that they have a healthy fear of God.

The foundation for the next global civilization will be based on the concept of *oneness*. This will result in societies based on love. Doesn't that sound better? It will be easy for people to accept a new spirituality based on love. People will begin to realize that the Bible has led them astray and away from God. Not only has the Bible led people astray, but society as well.

As previously stated, Western civilization is based on Christian values. Look at our current civilization. How does society currently perceive crime? Christians believe that crime is caused by evil people who have forsaken God and should be punished harshly. There is little compassion for criminals.

To New Agers, people who commit crimes are not perceived as evil but as reflections of society, as people who are catalysts for change. For instance, if someone is a thief, it is a reflection that he or she is not being provided for by society.

Granted, this is a difficult concept to grasp. It is hard to believe that criminals are equal to other members of society. We are so conditioned to believe in right and wrong that any concept alien to this is quickly rejected by the mainstream.

The only recourse is for these ideas to be relegated to the fringe of society.

In the New Age, a criminal will be perceived as someone who needs help, not someone who needs punishment. People will understand that we all have to live together. If one person needs help, that person will have help. What is a criminal other than someone who needs help and has rejected his community?

As stated earlier, Christians judge criminals harshly because of the belief in separation. Political leaders in the West who make the laws that decide the fate of criminals are a reflection of a Christian-dominated society. Society currently does not believe in rehabilitation. Thus, rehabilitation does not exist, or is rare.

I do not believe in political answers to our current problems. It is pointless to join political institutions and attempt change. Until society has transformed spiritually, our institutions and culture will not improve. They will, in fact, decay. I believe our institutions will continue to decay until they implode. I recommend that we all refuse to be involved in politics of any kind, and that we sit back and watch society collapse. Then we can start over.

Most people do not like to think too deeply about the foundations of society. For instance, the relationship between schools and Christian values is largely ignored. When I bring this up, people do not want to talk about it. "What's your point?" they ask. My point is that society is based on fallacies, and schools are the starting point for the continuation of these fallacies. What children are taught, and how they are conditioned, determines how a society will evolve.

School boards are locally elected and put in charge of educating our children. From my perspective, their role is to maintain and preserve the current system. The school boards are mainly made up of Christians, which is inevitable because America is at least 65 percent Christian. Christian values are the main criteria for the curriculum of our nation's schools, again reflecting pervasive societal values.

Look at the school system. When children first arrive in school at the tender age of five, they are conditioned to achieve and conform. There are no alternatives, except home schooling. Children must go to school and compete to make society and God proud of them.

If they do not want to learn what is being taught, they are in for a rough time. From this early age, they are taught that if they conform and achieve, they will be happy. Conversely, if they rebel against the expectations, happiness will be withheld. They are taught to achieve or else be ostracized. They are not given a choice. They are taught that only their achievements matter. If they do not accept this rule, they will be kicked out or disciplined. One reward for achieving is the honor roll; another is the ubiquitous "Student of the Month" bumper sticker that proclaims the accomplishments of students.

Another enticement to achievement is the opportunity to become involved in a school activity, such as a dramatic play or a sports team. Teachers make sure these "special" students feel happy about their achievements. It is not long before the students who are achievers begin to assert peer pressure on the non-achievers.

The rules are put into place at the school board level and are ironclad. Children who achieve and conform are rewarded with good grades and the possibility of college. Those who refuse to achieve and conform are shuffled along, and then pushed out into society ill-prepared.

When I say *pushed out*, I am talking about those who either drop out or graduate with a poor education. Hundreds of children and young adults drop out of school every day. Current graduation rates are less than 70 percent in the most prosperous country in the world. What is the response of the school boards? They claim it is not their responsibility and that all students are given an opportunity to graduate.

We treat the homeless and high school dropouts the same. We take away their dignity and place the blame on them. We often do the same thing to six-year-old children with their first report card. "Achieve or else," seems to be the motto of our society.

Do Christian values have anything to do with it? I think so. I think Christian values and Western civilization go hand in hand. Thus, when one falls, the other shall fall.

The school boards create this system of achievement based on current Western values. Is there really much difference between Christian values and Western values? I think there are very few differences between them. Some of my cousins went to a parochial school, and I went to a public school. Did we really have a different education? I do not think so.

Look deeper. The school system is very important to our society. Because of this importance, people with power have made sure that the school system meets society's needs. Thus, the school boards are accountable to the power brokers. The elite makes sure the school system is run a certain way. Political power is exerted to maintain the school system. School systems across the nation are pretty much the same because the same Western values dominate. You can ask people who have attended schools across the country what their schools were like and find little difference.

It is interesting that schools are run at the local level, yet are nearly uniform across the nation. What causes this uniformity? The answer, in my opinion, is Christian values.

We live in an achievement culture, and this culture is reinforced at an early age. The conditioning begins as early as a child's third year of age when they begin daycare. Then, grading in elementary school reinforces the conditioning of achievement. Is grading really necessary? Why can't kids just go to school and enjoy life? I find it amazing that the practice of grading is used so extensively, especially for young children. Does anyone realize the message being sent? Children who receive poor grades are denigrated. The message is that they are inferior.

Why talk about education? To make the point that Christian values are lacking. More than that, Christianity is the major reason why most of our institutions are failing.

Our current civilization must fall before the new civilization can take its place. If that is the case, we should try to understand why it is going to fail. This understanding will help us make the transition much more smoothly. If you see something coming, it is easier to prepare.

I feel kind of guilty writing so negatively about Christianity. Jesus was probably the greatest spiritual teacher ever on Earth, and he is closely identified with Christianity. His message, however, was not what Christianity evolved into. His message was love and simple ascetic living, not judgment and an opulent lifestyle. Moreover, Jesus was a Gnostic. He had a personal relationship with a higher power. I consider all New Agers to be Gnostics in the same sense as Jesus.

The foundation of Christianity is based on a false premise: separation. This false premise has actually caused the darkness and evil that is now upon the planet. How did this happen? Judgment leads to resentment, and resentment leads to hatred. We are locked into a vicious cycle of negativity. To break the cycle, we have to stop judging and begin allowing. Allowing leads to love, and love leads to harmony.

In the near future, people will begin to recognize the fallacy of separation. Soon, our institutions will begin to break down. The first to go will be the economic system. Next, the political system. Finally, the social system. Once this occurs, we will reflect on our beliefs and begin to make changes.

* * * * *

Our Western civilization and Christian values appear to be leading us toward a more complex society where technology continues to advance, and everyone competes against each other to achieve the American Dream. However, that is not our future. Instead, society is headed toward simpler times.

After a long period of economic decline, people will no longer feel compelled to focus on economic and material growth. Instead, the quest for economic advancement will slow, and a focus on creating a more humane society will unfold. People will become more concerned with their spirituality than their achievements. Our achievement obsession will decline as spirituality and humanity ascend in importance.

CHAPTER FOUR

Life is Difficult

I read somewhere recently that we are only 1 percent aware of what is occurring in our lives. I think this is possibly true because we are only vaguely aware of the interactions taking place in our lives on a subconscious level. We are not consciously aware of the inputs we are receiving or giving. Our information processing is limited, which leaves us oblivious to reality. This is why life on this planet is so difficult. To say the least, life is a challenge.

Life is difficult because we are not in our natural state. Our body is not *us*. It is just a body which is dependent on our consciousness. When we incarnate from the spiritual plane – where we do not have a physical body – to the physical plane, we literally take over a body. Then, when our lifetime is finished on Earth, we leave our body behind.

Life is difficult because we put on spiritual blinders, and accept the limitations of the physical plane when we inhabit a physical body. Moreover, we incarnate with only a fragment of our soul. This limits us further. These limitations trap everyone, whereby everyone's awareness is limited on this planet, some more than others. Awareness is limited to such an extent that if we did not have guides and a higher self, we could not exist.

We all have at least one spirit guide with us at all times. Without this guidance, we would experience a myriad of accidents and problems. The guidance from the spiritual plane to the physical plane occurs on a conscious and subconscious level. Because of this connection to the spiritual plane, everyone is more capable than it often appears, although still handicapped by the limitations of the physical plane.

Life is difficult even for those who are spiritually aware. Perhaps those few who are enlightened have an easy life, but that group is rare, and even they recognize the challenge of life on this planet. This is why old souls tend to be gentle to those with whom they interact. You can always recognize an aware old soul by his or her gentleness and spiritual wisdom.

For most people, just getting up in the morning and living through the day is a challenge. Often when we see handicapped people, we tend to empathize with their fate, but the fact is we are all handicapped. We might perceive that we have an advantage over a handicapped person, such as good health, all five senses, or all four limbs, but that advantage is an illusion. In a broader perspective, who is to know who has the advantage? What if their intuition is more highly developed? Or, if they are an advanced old soul?

I do not care how happy someone appears; his or her life is difficult and challenging. Everyone is trapped in limitation and facing some type of challenge. Material wealth, family, friends, fame, success, none of these can overcome our limitations. From a spiritual context, a homeless person and a movie star are equals, and they each have their own lessons. Moreover, each deserves our love and respect equally.

* * * * *

In order to counteract the difficulty of life, we should all prepare for what may come our way. For instance, we would not go on a backpacking expedition without planning and preparing. It is a good idea to meditate in the morning, do some type of prayer ritual (I recommend a hand prayer in several of my books, which I have been doing for years), and then plan our day. These simple steps can vastly improve our lives. The reason why we should do this is that we will be much more prepared for the day. Meditating and praying gets us in touch with our soul, and planning gets us focused on what we are going to do for the day.

I used to think planning was counterproductive, and that we should let our higher self guide us and live intuitively and spontaneously from minute to minute and day to day. Then, I started thinking about how I actually live. I came to the conclusion that I carefully plan my life. For instance, I can pretty much tell you what I am going to do for the next month, and especially for the next day. From this knowledge, I can use *intent* to direct that outcome and to hold closely to the plan. For instance, if it is Saturday, then I will be doing A, B, and C. My higher self and my guides can then schedule anything I have *not* planned and fit them into my plans. It is uncanny how everything flows and fits together.

Using our intent to expect a certain outcome helps us direct our lives. This kind of thought projection is what creates our lives. Likewise, what is the difference between intent and a plan? Are they not basically the same? If intent is vital to directing the outcomes in our lives, then plans are also directions. They allow us to conceptualize and visualize what we want in life. Do you remember the last chapter? Belief creates our reality.

I firmly believe that the only way to have harmony in our lives, and thus diminish the inherent difficulty in life, is to have a plan and firmly tell the Universe (God) what we expect (our intent). In fact, intent is everything. Intent coupled with belief directs the outcome of our lives.

Now, what I am about to say is not a contradiction to my previous statements. *I live by intuition.* In fact, my intuition tells me when to change my plan. Moreover, my expectations of my plan and my intuition work hand in hand. Thus, there is nothing contradictory about carefully planning and also being intuitively led. Indeed, this is how most spiritually minded people live.

In the morning, I do not always think about my daily plan. However, I do generally know what I am going to do that day, and what I am going to focus on. If someone calls me in the morning and asks me what I am going to do for that day, I generally will have an answer. I rarely live spontaneously throughout a day.

Why do all of this planning? Because I want the Universe to guide me and know where I want to go. Note that this is not a theory of mine. I have learned through research (mostly channeled material) that this is how the Universe works best. I am divine, and I have free will. I can choose my path in life, and the Universe will support it. In fact, the better my plan aligns with my blueprint (my life plan), the more the Universe will support me.

If my life plan is to be a writer and help humanity, then the Universe will help me achieve my goal. The Universe will be excited that I am carrying out my blueprint. The Universe (God, the Creator) wants me to have a plan. I have found that not having a plan and simply waiting for the Universe to miraculously change my life just leads to more waiting. The Universe wants us to figure it out. To repeat, the Universe wants us to be proactive and have a plan! How do I know this? First, by my research that says it's so. But, more importantly, by my experience. My life is multitudes more productive when I have a plan. And the quinky-dinks (odd coincidences), which prove to me I'm on the right path, come in waves.

When I know what I am going to do each day, my life flows more easily. When I have a plan, I feel prepared, and I feel supported by the Universe. I feel as if I am being proactive by choosing what I want to do. I literally tell the Universe with my intent, "This is what I am going to do today." Conversely, when I am spontaneous, anything can happen. I have found from experience that my life does not flow as well when I live spontaneously. In fact, when I do not have a plan, I often find myself bored and doing nothing. And life is too short to do nothing, especially when our goals do not manifest overnight, and usually take a lot of hard work.

In my opinion, to know where we are going, we have to have a plan. That plan may be for only a day or a year, but we need to be aware of our plan and our intent. Intuitively, we should understand our current situation. For instance, *why* are you working at your current job? *Who* are the people in your life? *How* are your finances, your health, your nutrition? All of these aspects of your life should be understood. You should be in charge of your life. Moreover, you should be taking active steps to improve it. For instance, if your nutrition is not improving from year to year, you are telling the Universe that you don't care about your health. That's not a good idea, because the Universe will give you exactly what you believe.

Perhaps I am naïve, but I consider myself healthy because I choose to be healthy. I use my intent and the Universe's help for that outcome. But this takes work. I have to eat well, take supplements, and exercise (which I have done since I started my spiritual path more than 30 years ago). The combination of intent, work, and planning makes it happen. I am being proactive, which is what the Universe demands. Again, life is hard!

Self-reliance and self-empowerment are about intent and belief. Do you know what you are doing in this lifetime? Are you confident that you are achieving it? If so, then you know who you are, and what your life is about. This awareness can make your life much easier than not having these answers. With these answers, you can plan your life accordingly.

To use the backpacking trip analogy again, the better prepared you are, the better the trip will go. It is that simple. Preparation includes why you want to go, where you are going, and how you are going to get there. Simply showing up unprepared and expecting the Universe to take care of you will not work, unless you are lucky enough to have a spouse or family member to take care of you.

We have to use our brains and our intuition (higher self). We have to take charge of our individual lives. This is what the coming Age of Aquarius is all about. People will need to be self-reliant. They will be expected to live in a proactive manner, to know who they are and where they are going. They will come to understand that survival and self-reliance go hand-in-hand. I say this harsh fact, because many will be leaving this planet early once the changes pick up speed.

When you live a proactive life, with the ability to lead yourself with plans and intent, you are very powerful. If you are prepared for the days ahead, no one can knock you off balance. Anyone can be a very powerful person. All one needs to do is know who one is (divine) and where one is going (your life plan). With these two beliefs, the Universe will support you and protect you.

Leading a proactive life has nothing to do with living up to the expectations of others. In fact, it is quite the opposite. You do not need to be successful in the eyes of others to be powerful. You can do anything you choose and still be successful in your own eyes (only you know your life plan). For instance, you can be a janitor or a waitress and be a very powerful person. The only relevant factor is how you feel about yourself.

I do not normally like to write about self-empowerment. I prefer for people to figure it out on their own. In fact, this is the first time I have written about it at length. I do not want people to think I can save them. The last thing I want is to be a self-help guru. *You* have to figure it out.

I do, however, want you to know you *can* feel empowered. Moreover, the more advanced your spiritual awareness, the more empowered you can become. It is not easy to obtain, and for most of us, it takes years of spiritual searching. If you are an old soul, however, your chances of success are high. This does not mean that life is going to get easy. We are still stuck with our limitations and that 1 percent awareness that I spoke of at the beginning of the chapter.

* * * * *

The way to make life easier is to be proactive. To be proactive, you must be aware of your current plan. You need to know what you are going to do tomorrow and what you are going to do next month. That is the first step. And when you know why you are doing it, then you will become empowered.

Haven't all the great spiritual teachers taught us to *know thyself?* This is indeed the secret to self-empowerment. Let me tell you a story. An elderly man who recently died is walking somewhere on the spiritual plane. He is feeling wonderful because he is in heaven. He is smiling and has a light step in his walk. He approaches a lady and asks for directions to see God. He is smug and implies that God will want to see him because he has lived a pious life and made every effort not to sin. He feels God will be proud of him and that he will be readily admitted into God's presence.

What happens? The lady asks the newly arrived soul to sit down beside her. Then she sincerely and with a warm heart proceeds to help the newly arrived soul to understand that *he* is God, that we are *all* God.

The newly arrived soul thought he had earned a right into heaven. In reality, he had lived his entire life in fear and judgment. He had looked around at a sinning society and judged everyone, thinking, *Oh, how God is going to be upset with all of you. Oh, how God is going to approve of my behavior!*

Let me tell another story. A robber is killed while committing an act of armed robbery. An angel arrives to take him to the higher planes, but the robber refuses to believe he is dead. The angel, very warmly and with love, asks the floating soul to look carefully at the dead body on the ground below. The angel gently tells him he has left his body, and the angel is there to take him to heaven. The soul is so shaken that he has difficulty believing or trusting the angel. Finally, the angel must leave, and the soul must decide if he wishes to go or stay. The soul decides that Satan would not offer a choice, so he goes with the angel. Before heading for a location on the higher planes, the soul asks the angel if he is in trouble. The angel smiles and says no.

From a spiritual standpoint, the souls in both of these two stories lacked spiritual awareness, and both needed to expand their awareness. They needed to grow spiritually. In fact, in their next lives, they could switch learning experiences.

You may be thinking I am wrong. How could a thief and a pious Christian be viewed as equals when their lives are over? That is how it works. All of us are equal in the eyes of God.

It is difficult to give up a belief in right and wrong. We want to feel good for being good, and we want to judge the bad guys. Accepting equality changes our lives dramatically. It is such a drastic change that most of us do not want to consider the possibility. However, this is a reality that must be faced.

The only important thing is to know yourself: who you are, what you believe, your strengths and weaknesses. Everything else is superfluous. You do not need to save the world, or anyone else, or achieve anything. Your only mission is to know yourself. When we know ourselves, we spread love in a natural and harmonious way – by following our life plan. This occurs because we are God. In essence, our plans are God's plans. Once we begin to realize who we are (God), our life changes in dramatic ways. In all likelihood, our plans will in some way, result in the spreading of love. When you look back on this lifetime (we all have a life review), you will look at it through the lens of love. How did you love others?

Why do you think the angels were so gentle and loving in the stories given above? The angels are souls like you and me. The only difference is spiritual awareness. They are not limited by the illusion of the physical plane. They know who they are and who we are. They are not confused, like we are. Have you ever heard stories of angels who scold or judge? No, because Angels are loving and nonjudgmental and hold unconditional love.

* * * * *

You may be wondering how can you remember who you are. Start by recognizing that the physical plane is an illusion. This is not *home* or where we come from.

Here are some "truths" to consider, many of which I have already mentioned.

- You are God.
- You have lived many lives, each bringing you closer to enlightenment.
- You carefully planned this life before you were born.
- You are not alone in carrying out your plan.
- You will not experience anything you do not want to experience.
- Your life is perfect.
- Everything is perfect.
- Everything happens for a reason.
- Nothing new can ever happen – everything happening has already happened.

After meditating on these truths, they will begin to seep into your consciousness. You can then begin paying attention to your current life plan. What does God want you to do in this lifetime? What makes your heart sing? What gives you passion? Connect with your spirit guides and higher self and ask about your plan. They will help you understand by giving subtle guidance. No longer will you feel alone in finding your way.

Connecting with our guides and higher self is quite real and possible. In my opinion, it is the only way to find out who we are. This is the connection to the source of life itself. It is also our connection with each other.

We need to feel our guides in our lives. We need to talk to them and ask them for guidance. This is the connection that empowers us. We can walk with a light step, with the awareness that we are being watched over and protected.

If you listen to your guides – using your intuition – they will tell you your plan. That is their job: to help you accomplish what you came into this life to do. Your plan was put into place before you were born. Once you grasp your plan, you can direct your life. You can make decisions for yourself based on your intuitive feelings. No longer do you have to follow society's lead. No longer do you have to feel powerless.

Most people feel powerless and are reactive instead of proactive. Most people allow society and other people to direct their lives. My guess is that about 80% of people follow the herd and prefer to be reactive followers. Your job is to now lead yourself in a proactive manner.

Spiritually aware people are proactive, directing their own lives by using their plans. For this reason, they are often judged as iconoclastic and strange. Currently, spiritually aware people are not respected for these traits, but this will soon change. People who are proactive and direct their own lives will be revered in the future. This is what the Age of Aquarius is all about: individualism (not nationalism), individual freedom (not national freedom), and self reliance (not interest groups). We each must know our plan and where we are going, not as a nation or group, but as an individual.

You might think we currently live in an era of individualism and freedom, but that is not the case. Today we live in an era of the interest *group*. We have national freedom, where freedom is codified for all Americans. You might say we have equal freedom, but not individual freedom. We have national individualism in which individualism correlates with national values. Most people identify with an interest group and do what is expected of that group.

Group behavior dominates America today. People act according to a particular interest group's behavior. For instance, if you are affluent and White, you likely hold certain values and believe certain truths. These values and truths allow you to be a member of that group, thus giving you an identity. Political parties and religions are other forms of group behavior and identities.

Today, just about everyone identifies with a group. In the near future, this concept of group behavior will break down, especially religions. The Aquarian is an individualist, a person who can fit in anywhere yet refuses to be defined. The Aquarian loves to shock people with the unconventional, which is at odds with our current interest group behavior. Today, everyone is expected to abide by certain behaviors. Just try to break the dress code at work and see if anybody notices.

What I have been talking about throughout this chapter is individualism and self-reliance, which are the opposite of group behavior. When you begin to live by your own values and beliefs, without worrying about how others perceive those values, you are becoming self-reliant. You no longer feel the need to satisfy the expectations of others. Instead, you satisfy your own expectations: your life plan. And this makes life easier.

You may have noticed that this concept is revolutionary. True individualism abandons government power, which requires political parties. So, how can society work? How can we be governed without government power? I have to smile, knowing that true freedom can exist only when political parties do not exist, which is where we are going as a civilization. Thus, national government will not last much longer. Slowly, steadily, as spiritual awareness expands on this planet, governing bodies will lose their power over individuals.

* * * * *

When we identify with a group, we give up our power to that group by adhering to the group's beliefs and values. Conversely, when you adhere to your *own* beliefs, you are self-empowered. This is truly a new way of living versus the current norm. Yes, some people are self-empowered today, but they are not the norm. Soon, there will be a trend toward self-empowerment, leading to a civilization based on individual self-empowerment. Note that when I speak of self-empowerment, I am talking about people who hold their own beliefs and values – they do not identify with a group.

A new world is dawning in which group beliefs will not be as important as an individual's beliefs. For instance, religions will steadily wither away as the group beliefs they espouse become irrelevant. Each individual will have his or her own unique beliefs and spirituality. Spirituality will be Gnostic, with a direct link to God and a personal relationship with God, without any third party or religious dogma creating that link.

Once I became spiritually aware and recognized that *all* are one, I have not belonged to any separate group, including any religious or political organizations. All I need is my connection to Spirit, and that is all I will ever need. My connection to Spirit is the true group connection. I feel connected to everyone. Joining a group would only cause conflict by creating an identification with a group and not the whole.

How can you be free to follow your life's plan if you identify with a group? We each have a unique life plan, which is not known to us in its entirety. To achieve it, you must be free of restraints that keep you from following your intuition, as free as you possibly can be, and ready to follow your higher self. Anything that restricts your freedom is a potential restriction to your life's plan. Thus, if you really want to be free, do not affiliate with a group.

The best way to help humanity is to shine your light by setting an example. This does not mean you need to tell anyone else how to live. You do not need to join an organization or attempt to save the planet, although if you feel led, then go for it. All you really need to do is be an example.

Change happens when people change. First, a few individuals begin connecting to their souls and become self-reliant individualists who live intuitively. Then, others become aware of these individuals and also begin to live intuitively. This leads to a steady evolutionary change. Eventually, the majority of the population will become self-reliant individualists who live by their own beliefs and values. The result will be a civilization based on oneness and true freedom.

It is interesting to note that Aquarians generally refuse to belong to a group. They also generally refuse to identify people as belonging to a group. The Aquarian sees everyone from the perspective of equality. Members from diverse groups are equal in their eyes. To them a Nazi and a priest are equal; they both are *people*.

It is also interesting to note that Aquarians have strong desires for personal freedom. As far as Aquarians are concerned, if they do not have the freedom to search for truth, life is not worth living. Moreover, if everyone does not have the same personal freedom, life is not fair. The Aquarian desires peace and freedom, brotherly love and equality. These are the traits of the next civilization in the not-too-distant future.

Aquarians are nice. It is their nature to be friendly. In the Age of Aquarius, people will be nice to each other. This is quite a change from the current state of society. Once we finish the transition into the Age of Aquarius, life will not be as difficult. I am optimistic that life will be easier as everyone becomes spiritually aware.

- Some helpful advice to make your life easier.
- Do not take life too seriously.
- Walk with a light step and an easy smile.
- Be kind and generous.
- Love everyone.
- Relish each day.
- Be happy.
- Trust the Universe to only give you what you need.
- Have a plan.
- Find something to do that you enjoy.

Happiness makes life easier. *Webster's Dictionary* defines happiness as having, showing, or causing a feeling of great pleasure, contentment, joy. I believe happiness is contentment with our lives. I also believe that contentment is a perception, and thus, happiness is a *choice*. Anyone can choose to be grateful for one's life, which is a form of contentment. Thus, happiness is a self-created state of mind. The *feeling* of happiness is our own creation. I cannot tell you how to create happiness in your life. That is up to you, but I do firmly believe spiritual awareness will increase your happiness.

Spiritual awareness has other benefits. For instance, it leads to more enthusiasm for life. By understanding who you are (God), and that your life is perfect, you cannot help but become more enthusiastic. Once enthusiasm appears in your life, each day is filled with anticipation. You no longer require extra excitement from the many temptations that exist today.

No longer is life perceived as mundane and boring, and in need of stimulation or escape.

* * * * *

Our lives are guided by spiritual forces greater than ourselves – our higher self, our guides, God. They know what we came to learn, and they gently lead us into experiences that will teach us. When we acknowledge and interact with these forces, we experience life in a more profound way. In fact, every day can feel somewhat miraculous.

In the early 1990s, when working in Los Angeles, I kept noticing this guy during lunch. I did not know anyone, so I always ate alone. Initially, we did not talk, but I felt a spark of recognition. And because we did not talk, the lunch periods seemed uneventful. Then, one day, after nearly *two* years, he approached me.

All this time, I had perceived the lunch period to be an uneventful experience. It turned out that he was a spiritual person and was interested in reading one of my books. After he read the first one, we talked and became friends. I became a bit of a spiritual mentor to him, and I think I had a positive impact on his life.

Our everyday experiences are often more important than we realize. Little events can have enormous significance. Life is difficult, but we are learning much more than we perceive.

* * * * *

This was a long chapter. Thanks for sticking it out. In closing, I want to share some knowledge that not many know. The real reason life is so hard is that most people trap themselves. You are probably doing this to yourself and are not aware of it. We trap ourselves in a variety of ways, but it really comes down to one thing: we project the belief in separation and that we are not divine, or that someone else is not divine.

When we project separation, the Universe recognizes that we are not spiritually aware, and it gives us what we believe. And guess what that means? A lower frequency. Why? Because only spiritually aware people have a high frequency. You earn your frequency. It doesn't come to us by grace. So, by projecting separation, we trap ourselves in the same frequency and can't grow spiritually. That's not a good thing today when our frequency is the difference between living and dying.

The good news is that by reading this book, you should learn how not to trap yourself. The frequency of love is the ideal method. If you do that, then you will vibrate at a higher frequency, and possibly join the 100,000 cycles per second club.

CHAPTER FIVE

Harmlessness

There is no randomness in life. Everything happens for a reason. Moreover, every aspect of our lives was pre-planned and is predicated by our beliefs. Our beliefs are like magnets drawing us to experiences. That is why our lives are perfect. We are getting exactly what we believe.

Most people do not accept this concept. Most look at their lives as a series of random events. There is, however, order in our lives. In fact, all of the potential experiences that are possible have already happened. Life is very much like a computer simulation that has already taken place. This is why randomness and God's plan for our lives are completely at odds with each other.

Within God's grand plan are the myriad of plans that each of us has made. What brings the grand plan to life is our beliefs, which are all pre-programmed. Our beliefs are not created after we are born, but before. We bring them with us from our soul. Some of our beliefs are hidden and need to be awakened, but the potential has been pre-planned in advance.

Once we realize that we are creating our own life through our beliefs, we can accept it. From that point of acceptance, we can be harmless to ourselves and to society. We can forgive ourselves and anyone who has done us harm and go forward with our lives. Moreover, no matter what we have created to this point in our lives, or will create in the future, we can accept it as perfect. We begin to understand that not only are our lives enough, but they are exactly what we need. The Rolling Stones had it right. We might not get what we want, but we get what we need.

Once we get to this point of spiritual awareness, harmlessness becomes possible. We become aware that everyone's life is perfect, and then act in accordance with that realization. We come to the recognition that the world is divinely ordered. Once this recognition is real to us, we become a force for peace on the planet. And once enough people come to this recognition, the planet becomes peaceful. This is why war will soon go away.

* * * * *

Harmlessness is a state of being. We no longer need to identify with our egos. Instead of competing with others and forcing our will upon them, we allow others their freedom.

Harmlessness is a state of cooperation. It is the opposite of trying to control someone. It is recognizing that everyone is trying as hard as they can, and they are sovereign beings. But more than that, it is recognizing that they are aspects of God who deserve our respect. Not because they have earned it – that is how old thinking – but because they exist.

By being harmless, we are loving others unconditionally and allowing them to live as they see fit. We are aware that the ego personalities that people reflect are an illusion, and that the true self of each person is much more than apparent.

As evolved souls, our job is to shine our light by setting an example of being harmless. That way, when people are looking for understanding after society deteriorates, we can be there to help. Kryon, who is channeled by Lee Carroll, likes to call evolved souls *lighthouses*. Evolved souls carry an enormous amount of light that needs to be shared with the world. This is why New Agers are also called *Lightworkers*. The light that they work with does not come from electricity, but is instead the essence of God, which is pure energy. Lightworkers project their light out to the world simply by being, and many of them are healers and work directly with this light, which is energy.

Note: Our soul is pure energy, and when we leave our bodies, we become light beings. On the etheric planes, we shine as light because we are pure energy. We don't need an energy source. We are the energy source.

Most people struggle with their lives. Moreover, they do not feel there is enough love in their lives. From this absence of love – in the face of struggle – they are constantly looking to others for a shred of unconditional love that they so desperately desire. This is where harmlessness comes in because we can provide that unconditional love.

When we stand before someone without judgment, with only unconditional love, he or she can feel our support and empathy. This acknowledgment goes further when we are consistently harmless. By being harmless, we offer the kind of support and care that people can trust.

We all need to be harmless to get along in a utopian society, which is what we are creating. Although we may not have a utopian society today, that does not mean we cannot aspire toward that eventual outcome. For instance, when the doorbell rings and there stands a person in need, the harmless person responds in a positive way and does not inflict additional pain.

Each of us has incredible opportunities to add love and light to this world. We constantly have opportunities to affect other people's lives in positive ways. Being harmless allows us to seize these opportunities.

We constantly receive responses from people with whom we interact. This interaction affects us as well as them. If we are harmless, the ramifications likely have a positive outcome. Conversely, if we are not harmless, we can create a negative outcome.

The last thing people need when they are struggling is for others to make their lives more difficult. Yet, this is what everyone seems to do. People are mean to each other. Most refuse to allow others to live as they want. In essence, people are harmful to each other.

Instead of being harmless, most people are harmful. In today's society, no one can do anything without other people judging their actions. We live in a culture of conditional love, and any deviation from expected roles is judged harshly. How many of us are trying to live up to the expectations of family and peers?

Being harmless is allowing people to live as they choose and supporting their choices: not only the choices we agree with but *all of their choices*. This is a radical idea in our current society in which the concepts of right and wrong are so highly valued. I am suggesting that we support *all* choices. Not just the choice to be a doctor, but the choice to be a janitor or an unsuccessful artist.

How many people are in prison today because their family and friends withheld support for their choices? Choices such as which friends to have, which clothes to wear, which lines of work to pursue. How many criminals started down the road to crime as angry teenagers because people refused to accept their choices? Is it their fault their anger and alienation led to criminal behavior? No. If they had been loved by society, crime might not have happened.

Maybe I am wrong on this point, but I believe I am a lot closer to the truth than the current condemnation of criminals. I know my ideas are not widely accepted at this time. I also know the reason I incarnated was to shake people up. The coming civilization will be much closer to these ideas than the current prevailing beliefs.

* * * * *

At the heart of harmlessness is unconditional love. When we understand each soul is perfect and does not need to do anything to achieve salvation, we are able to love each person without condition. Conditional love – the love that is prevalent in society today – is based on achievement and behavior. The belief in conditional love prevents people from being harmless.

Here is an example of what I mean by harmlessness. A lady at work changes her hair length from medium to short. Instead of allowing her to have the new hairstyle with little notice, people make a big thing of it. Those who like it smile and give her a compliment, whereas others grimace or snicker. Instead of being harmless, the co-workers are harmful. They cannot help themselves from judging her.

People are so caught up in their false personalities (egos) that any change to their environment is perceived as a threat. To maintain their identities, they threaten others with emotional trauma – if they dare to break from the norm. People are like policemen, always on the lookout for violators. Even worse, people are vigilantes, enforcing the law at their whim. ("Look, his shirt is wrinkled. My goodness, you would think he would know better!")

Ego causes people to harm each other constantly – not physically, but emotionally. As mentioned previously, instead of being harmless, most people are harmful. Why do people like to "stick in the knife" with a verbal barb? And I am not just talking about saying it to the victim's face. I am talking about gossip, which is pervasive in society.

Do we really think we can say something about someone else without ramifications? Every word we utter and every thought we think has ramifications and consequences. Not only that, but every word is recorded, and everyone has access to this record. Those people you talk about have access to your thoughts – after this life is over, and they review their past life in the Akashic records.

Look at the ramifications of gossip. Words have power, more than we perceive. When we talk about people in a negative way, we harm them. Did that sentence hit home? You do not believe me? You think idle chat about other people is harmless? To the contrary, thought has power because thought is energy. Words are as real as physical force. Is that not what gossip is? A verbal attack? Words and thoughts have power. Think about it.

People talk about each other because they identify with their own personalities. Most people think their personalities are real, and that their current personalities are their true identities. The fact is, the current personality is an illusion. In fact, it is fake. It is only a temporary personality being used for this lifetime. Thus, the identities that people perceive as real are not so real.

To make an analogy, life is like a theatrical play. Everyone is playing a role, and that role is the personality. To get an idea of how this works, think of Al Pacino, the actor. You have probably seen him in numerous roles in several movies. However, if you met him on the street, would you know him? No. Instead, you would identify him with the personalities he has played, even though they were only roles.

Our true self is spirit. Our true self is a *compilation* of the many incarnations (roles) and experiences we have had. When we shed the personality of this present life (at the end of this lifetime), our spirit appears. Our spirit identity is much different than our physical personality role. This is why we are more than we appear. A pauper has been a king, a king a pauper.

Most people identify strongly with their personality because they believe it is real. From this belief, people are constantly defining their identity. People believe their identity is all they have, and they feel a compulsion to constantly define themselves, as well as to defend the identity they have created.

This compulsion is the source of harm because people are constantly defining themselves by comparing their identity with others. This is why people talk about other people and judge other people. People think they are real, and they feel compelled to define their reality.

I call it a source of harm because it is the opposite of harmlessness. Instead of allowing and thus spreading love, people withhold love and spread judgment. When people identify with their personalities, they feel compelled to attack those who impinge on their identities. People create their own little worlds in order to define themselves, and then they defend those beliefs.

Instead of being aware that life is a play, and we are all actors, people think the personality – Earthly identity – is real. From this belief, they spend all of their time defining their personalities. Instead of realizing that God is in charge of the destiny of this planet, they think they are in charge of their own little worlds. Thus, people subvert God's will by following their own wills (egos). In essence, people have lost touch with God, and they do not know how to be harmless.

This is why there is so much darkness on the planet at this time. Let me give an example. Recently, an eleven-year-old boy was murdered in Chicago. His name was Yummy Sandifer. His death made national news, and his photograph appeared on the cover of *Time* magazine. What made his murder national news was that he himself had been wanted for murder, and he was only *eleven* years old. Yummy had averaged one felony per month since the age of ten. He had stolen cars (he could drive proficiently), carried a gun, rarely attended school, and was known as a violent criminal.

In the large inner cities of America, such as Los Angeles, New York, Detroit, St. Louis, and Chicago, was this boy that unique? The answer is no. Why do so many young boys get into so much trouble? The answer is the beliefs of society. Yes, they create their individual lives, but what alternatives do they have? People have constantly harmed them from birth, both emotionally and physically.

From this constant barrage of attacks, their only recourse has been to respond. They are responding to their environment. If you think this eleven-year-old boy would have turned out the same if he had been raised in the suburbs with loving parents, you are mistaken. And he is no different from the myriad of children who end up in police stations every day. They are responding!

What are they responding to? As I have said, they are responding to the constant harm being inflicted upon them. We are not talking about a few people harming these children. We are talking about *everyone* with whom they come into contact, except the occasional aware old soul who crosses their path and gives them a welcoming smile.

The intensity of harm taking place in the inner cities is overwhelming and has led to prevalent drug use that is devastating to the lower classes, who are exposed to the most harm. Why is this happening? Because the people in the inner cities expect more out of life. They see the quality of life that surrounds them, and they compare it to their own. They do not realize that their lives are perfect. As a consequence, they are not satisfied. Instead of recognizing God's will, they only perceive their own will, and this has led to a lot of emotional pain.

As I have said, most people do not accept their lives as perfect. From this perspective, people in the inner cities are not satisfied with their lives. Their beliefs are focused on the negative, and that is what they get. The result is they harm each other. Instead of living with joy in their hearts – realizing that each of us is divine – they live with anger, anxiety, and desire.

Whereas people who live in the suburbs use the illusion of material comfort to make themselves feel happy, people in the inner cities do not have this crutch. They are left with the feeling that life is not fair. They are left with the bitterness of having little in an affluent society.

In the inner city, nearly everyone is unsatisfied. They want more out of life than poverty and deprivation. This desire is from personal will and is a rejection of God's will. The result is a pervasive denial of God. The ego reigns in this environment.

In today's culture, people believe that the pursuit of happiness is the only option. People live to satisfy their personal dreams and desires. From this perspective, they live for themselves. They follow *their* will to satisfy *their* needs.

The pursuit of happiness is often a denial of God's will. Why? Because it often implies a lack of satisfaction and contentment with what God has provided. Today, most people believe happiness can be found through satisfying dreams and desires. And because people in the inner cities have the hardest time fulfilling their dreams and desires, they have the hardest time finding happiness – not knowing that happiness is a choice.

Whereas the inner cities reflect the extreme harm taking place today, the suburbs reflect the inner cities. Everything happening in the inner cities is also occurring everywhere else on a smaller scale. People in the suburbs lack spiritual awareness to the same degree. The only difference is that the lack of spiritual awareness is more intense in the inner cities – beliefs are more acutely skewed to the negative.

When children grow up in the inner cities, they are forced to play negative roles at an early age, roles such as being mean to other children, stealing, or fighting for their life. These roles are a natural byproduct of their environment. It is as natural for a boy to commit a crime in the inner city as it is for a boy in the suburbs to do his homework. They are both playing the roles their environment provides.

Sure, they have choices. Not all boys in inner cities commit crimes, and not all boys in suburbs do their homework. My point is the environment provides the opportunity for choices. If it were not for the harm constantly inflicted, they would not choose negative roles.

In the inner cities, judgments are intensified, and thus, harm is intensified. People are so caught up in following their own will in order to satisfy their dreams and desires, that they lose sight of God. People judge each other constantly in order to find a reason why their dreams and desires are unfulfilled.

The inner cities are the extreme, but they display what is occurring throughout society. If people are going to be harmless, then beliefs have to change. The beliefs that people hold today are creating conflict, division, anxiety, fear, and negativity. These beliefs are no longer tenable for the survival of the human race. Instead, we are going to create a new civilization based on new beliefs. We will focus on the needs of humanity: peace, freedom, equality, compassion, caring, and love. This will come about when we recognize the oneness of life and our inherent divinity. Only then can we become harmless to one another.

Chapter Six

Human Interaction

Finding God is what life is about – even if you are not looking – and human interaction is how we do it. By sharing our lives, we come to know the concept of love. And from love, we come to know God.

Love is the key to spiritual awareness. Why? Because it's the core of the soul, and really all the soul cares about. When we get close to love, we get close to God. So, from a spiritual context, our human interactions are the most important aspects of our lives.

When we do our life review, very little will have to do with what we did while we were alone. Unless, perhaps, you were handicapped, and your struggles were done alone. But for most of us, our life review will focus on how we interacted with others.

How we interact with each other is the focal point of our learning experiences while on Earth. What we will remember after returning *Home* were our relationships with others. These are the events in our lives that are indelibly stamped on our souls and occur through human interaction.

Anytime we interact with another person, there is a purpose and meaning behind it. In other words, each interaction has a context. Not only is there a context, but there is also an outcome. How we act and react in every situation has a bearing on our souls. One event in this lifetime can dictate other events in this lifetime or the next. Little things can have huge consequences.

Once we recognize the significance of human interaction, all human contact takes on a new perspective. Then our life becomes much more spiritual. We begin to see others as spiritual beings who deserve our respect. Judgment becomes a thing of the past because we see everyone as our spiritual equal.

Human contact represents an opportunity for us to understand ourselves better. Not only are human interactions opportunities, they are the very experiences we need because, as stated, experience, more than anything else, propels our spiritual growth. Once we are consciously aware of the significance of human interaction, each human contact takes on more meaning. We become aware that the little things are important, and that how we treat others literally creates our karma and future experiences. We become nice people.

Most people deny the importance of our human interactions, and thus think it is acceptable to be rude to those they don't like. As a culture, we generally take life in stride and nonchalantly ignore the significance of our daily interactions. Instead of living consciously aware of the events in our lives as significant, we live with a lack of awareness. Instead of being gentle, empathetic, and understanding, we fail to make a connection with others.

As I have previously stated, life is like a play. The only difference is that in a play, actors are aware they are acting. In life, only enlightened people are aware they are playing a role. As we become enlightened, we begin to realize that everyone is playing a role. We wake up to the awareness that we are all God in various disguises.

Once we realize this, life changes. For instance, when we recognize that others are playing roles, it is pointless to get angry or judgmental toward them. James Earl Jones was Darth Vader's voice, but no one resents him for it. Likewise, no one in heaven resents the soul who played Hitler.

As we evolve in our spiritual awareness, we become more compassionate and understanding, instead of reacting negatively. We learn to allow people to create their lives as they see fit and applaud them for their efforts. Today, this is uncommon and the exception. Today, we only applaud those whom society deems worthy of applause.

When we do not react in a negative manner toward people, our life begins to take on a magical quality. The people in our lives begin to reciprocate with love and compassion (the higher you align, the more you shine). In fact, miracles happen. This is hard to explain in words, but when we are compassionate with each other, God gets involved and blesses the situation (if you bless others, you are blessed in return). Conversely, when we react negatively, God steps aside and allows us to make a mess of our lives (if you damn another, you are damning yourself). God's grace is real, but it doesn't happen on its own. Instead, we manifest it in our lives by how we interact with each other (or, how we interact with humanity).

By knowing that others are playing roles, we have a distinct advantage over those who are caught in the illusion of life. They can try to disrupt our lives, but we can see through it. For instance, we can consciously realize their anger is based on what they perceive to be real. We can recognize the role they are playing and refuse to play along with them (we can rise above their charade and see through it).

By not getting upset and not reacting in anger, we are sending love to people. In fact, the best way to not get upset is to react with compassion and empathy for their plight (and naivety). We do not have to react and play the character they want us to play. We do not have to go along. We can refuse. In their minds, they think life is real. In your mind, you can realize life is a charade … and not react.

There are two kinds of people: those who know they are incarnated and are playing a role (gnostics) and those who do not (non-gnostics). The first type does not give us many problems or challenging situations. However, many of the second type love to push our buttons, so confrontations are bound to occur. These situations can be diffused by not reacting – by not getting into character. When a confrontation arises, if we do not react, we are able to send love and compassion.

How do you send love to others? By perceiving their lives as perfect. Honor them by acknowledging their divinity. Perceive them as God, even if they do not. Allow people to live their lives as they choose. This perception toward others is what enlightenment is all about.

People who are enlightened think of other people's lives as perfect. Everyone is getting exactly what they need. This, of course, does not mean we should be callous, but quite the opposite. If someone is floundering and struggling, we should do what we can to help them. During their period of struggle, we should not demean them in any way. However, an enlightened person knows that there are lessons to be learned from those difficult experiences.

* * * * *

With conscious effort (spiritual practice), our awareness can be expanded to live from an enlightened perspective. This change takes our lives in a whole new direction. We think differently, react differently, and definitely live differently. Everything changes. As my sisters like to say, "That's not the brother I grew up with!"

We are approaching an enlightened age. Duality is no longer needed on this planet and soon will be replaced with the concept of oneness. This incredible transformation will change human interaction in a revolutionary manner. Lightworkers – those spiritually aware people who are helping humanity evolve – are ahead of the curve. They are setting an example for others to follow.

When we come to the realization that everyone is *one*, we will no longer accept others on a conditional basis. We will be able to love everyone as is. This perception is what will transform society. People will begin loving each other. Human interactions will change in a dramatic manner. Instead of approaching someone as if they are a stranger, we will approach them as if we are family.

Love will flow as people acknowledge divinity in each other. Love is something that has power all on its own (love God with all your heart and watch the magic in your life unfold). Love is a power that overwhelms people. Love is the core of our being and is an aspect of everyone's consciousness – it is our source. We can all relate to each other with love. Love is the universal language.

The fastest way to develop spiritual awareness is through love. Spiritual awareness correlates directly with love consciousness. You can do this in a number of ways: through serving humanity, in personal relationships, and even by simple acts of kindness. Most of these occur through human interaction, although some serve all of humanity as lightworkers (through podcasts, writing, and even sending light energy to the planet and humanity).

After love begins to flourish on the planet, the next step will be the expanded usage of unconditional love. Unconditional love comes from the awareness that everything is God, and everything is perfect. From this awareness comes the understanding to allow others to make their own choices. Instead of forcing our will on others, we no longer judge them. We *allow*. We shine our light and allow others to do as they desire.

One of the hardest things to do is to allow. Try saying this to someone you love and mean it: "I love you unconditionally. You can do whatever you want. I *allow* you to create your life as you see fit."

Unconditional love will have an enormous impact on human interaction. We will no longer try to tell others how to live. That is their choice. This will become a new challenge for adults raising their children. Parenting will change dramatically. How do you parent a divine child whose life is perfect? (Read my book *Conversations with an Immortal*).

To allow is to love. Because everyone is God, telling someone else how to live is tantamount to giving God guidance. If someone asks, fine. Otherwise, leave them to their own choices.

Everyone is learning through their experiences. That is the perception we need to develop. When we recognize that everyone is learning, allowing becomes natural. We no longer feel the need to show everyone else our idea of the right way. We recognize that *all* ways are right ways.

What about crime and self-destructive behaviors? What about abusive behavior or child neglect? Are these not wrong? No, they are not. God is never wrong. God can't be wrong, because God is perfect. God is simply experiencing the infinite. Judging something as wrong is from a limited perception of reality. Someone with a larger view of reality has a different perception. When people choose negative experiences, their motives are not always apparent.

Morality is never black and white. Negative experiences can be just as valuable as positive ones for the soul. The more you cringe at this fact, the more tightly connected you are to your ego, which is an illusion. The ego wants you to judge right and wrong. That is one of its favorite buttons to push.

* * * * *

We allow others to make their own choices because we know they are creating their own realities, and that no one's life is random. There are no accidents. Every moment happens by design. Every moment in someone's life directly correlates to his or her beliefs.

The next time you are interacting with someone you perceive to have a problem, ask yourself: Do they really need your help, or did they create this experience for a reason? Quite likely, their *perceived* problem is leading them where they need to be.

CHAPTER SEVEN

The Details Are What Count

Virgo is the astrological sign that notices details. The average Virgo is aware of every little detail. To a Virgo, it is the details that are important. The average Virgo takes the little things more seriously than the rest of us. If you invite a Virgo to dinner, he or she will notice everything in your house, from dust on the TV to your crooked pictures on the wall.

We all have a Virgo consciousness to a certain degree, and each of us can use this consciousness to pay closer attention to the details in our lives. You can use your Virgo consciousness to become a spiritual being – someone who is guided internally and attuned to your higher self.

By paying attention to the details in your life, you can learn what the inner world is trying to tell you. Make no mistake, you are influenced and guided by your higher self from the inner world. Ideally, you want to form a close relationship with this guidance. In fact, to become a spiritual being, you must work in tandem with your spirit guides and higher self.

Ignoring the inner world and focusing on the physical world is a perfectly valid experience. However, we are entering an era where that no longer works. In the near future, those who try to rely on their ego will find that their lives are falling apart and no longer working. So, you will need to learn how to become a spiritual being who is closely connected to their internal guidance. Without this guidance, your life will become a mess.

How do you do it? How do you connect with your guides and become inner-directed? I wrote a book called *Finding Your Soul,* as well as an accompanying workbook. I will give you the short version.

I spoke about this earlier when I talked about quieting your mind. The pathway to your soul (higher self) and spirit guides is only open when your mind is quiet. Let me show you an easy method of opening that gateway. All you have to do is feel your hands. When you feel the tingling, the gateway will open, and you will notice that your mind is quiet. This is basically a short meditation. Another way to do it is to pay attention to your breathing.

Once that gateway is open, begin to observe your thoughts. Become the observer and ignore your thoughts. The observer is your soul. It is not your ego. You have just learned how to separate your ego from your soul. Practice doing this daily. Become aware of the difference and get closer to your soul.

The observer (your soul) does not have emotion. That is how you know the difference. The ego generates emotion. Let me give you a couple of examples so you will understand.

Let's say you come home from work, and two family members are screaming at each other, and both are angry. Your ego is going to push your buttons and get you to become emotional. However, you have another option. You can stand back and detach and become an observer. You can quiet your mind and wonder why they are arguing, knowing that it has a purpose and that you don't have to control the outcome. It's not your argument. It's theirs. You can be extremely gentle because the soul does not get emotional. Why not? Because it is just a communication channel.

The more you can learn to be the observer with a quiet mind, the closer you will get to your spirit guides and higher self. Why? Because when you become the observer of your thoughts, you are opening the channel. Trust me when I say that they – your spirit guides and higher self – will begin communicating with you.

I have one more example. Do you know what happens when people have an NDE (near-death experience)? Their soul pops out of their body. Then they have some type of experience (often extraordinary), and finally pop back into their body. After the NDE, they are profoundly changed from experiencing their soul. They experience it as pure energy. What spins their noodle is that even though they don't have a brain, eyes, or ears, their soul can think, hear, and see when it is out of the body. Also, their identity is intact. They feel like themselves (with a complete memory of their life), albeit without an ego.

Thus, our soul consciousness is an identity that we brought with us when we incarnated. The ego is a quasi-personality consciousness that is created for this lifetime and is embedded with the soul. These two consciousnesses interact for this lifetime. The ego-personality does not come with us when the soul leaves the body. The ego is made up of our horoscope, numerology, parental beliefs and influences, societal beliefs and influences, and several other factors, including our soul blueprint.

So, our soul is our true self, and the ego is our false self. We want to get closer to our soul and have a relationship with it and our spirit guides. It is weird at first and can be something that is difficult to share with others. For instance, when you tell someone your soul wants you to do this or that, they might think you are a wee bit strange.

My soul tells me when to write a new book, including the title and often the skeleton of the plot. How do I know it is my soul? Because they argue with me if I say no and won't take no for an answer. You may think my brain is playing tricks on me, but does your brain argue with you? Once you begin communicating with your soul, you will know what I am talking about.

So, step one is learning how to observe your thoughts and bring your soul into your life. Step two is to acknowledge that your soul exists, and that it exists on a higher spiritual plane. By acknowledging the spiritual plane, you expose it. For instance, when you go shopping, how often do you forget something? The secret is to never shop alone. I do not mean with another person; I mean with your spirit guides. If you ask your guides for help, they will tell you what you need, or what you forgot. This may sound crazy, but try it. Before you walk into a store, ask your guides what you need. Then, before you leave, ask if you forgot anything. Listen carefully. They will tell you. They like to talk. They use telepathy.

The more you talk to your guides, the more you will be able to hear them. Sometimes it will be a voice in your head, but more often, it is an impulse or feeling. How this communication takes place is through our integrated consciousness. Our higher self and guides are literally part of our consciousness. After a while, you never feel alone again.

This is *real* communication with another consciousness – your higher self – and not just with your own mind. I know this from experience. For instance, my mind could not possibly know that a car was coming from my right, when a voice in my head distinctly yelled to me, *Look to the right!* Or when I am walking past the cat food in a store and hear,

Cat food. They do that all the time. After a while, you just laugh. They can have quite a sense of humor. I often say, "No laughing," when I do something stupid. I've literally said that dozens of times. Not because they laugh at me (they don't), but because I *know* they witnessed it. So, it's kind of an inside joke when I say, "No laughing." It's also an opportunity for me to let them know that I know they are with me.

I often have short conversations with them. This can occur when I ask them questions, but usually, they will initiate it. You will quickly learn that you are not talking to yourself. My sister told me she talks to herself. In actuality, she is talking to her guides and doesn't realize it.

Whenever you drive your car, ask your guides to take care of you. There is no reason to consciously drive alone, when in fact, we are not alone. I talk to my spirit guide, Joe (he's been with me since I was born) when I am driving. From experience, I know he is always with me. I have not had an accident since I started acknowledging Joe. Also, I have avoided several accidents because of his help (*Look to the right!*).

By paying attention to the details in life and living in the present moment, such as how the car in front of you is driving, you can receive guidance. From experience, I know that by paying attention and being an observer, it is easier for my guides to communicate with me. The more I notice, the more they can help. Noticing little things makes a big difference with their communication. The key is to not always be on autopilot. That is what the ego wants you to do. Get out of autopilot mode and become more aware of the present moment as a conscious observer.

For instance, I am much more productive if I am focused with an observant mind. However, if I am thinking about several things at once, my productivity bogs down. Also, if my mind is racing too fast, then I can't hear my spirit guides. However, as long as I have an observant mind, my guides make sure that I take care of the important things. This makes my life much more harmonious and flowing.

Is communicating with the unseen schizophrenia? Hardly. The inner world is much more real than the outer world, which is a façade. Connecting with the inner world is the way of a spiritual being. Most people (that will change soon!) rarely perceive interaction with the spiritual plane of existence, although it is taking place. Everyone is being guided to a certain extent.

Our higher self and spirit guides all exist on the spiritual plane. By acknowledging that they exist and influence your life, you can use their influence in a positive way. More than that, you become a spiritual being by using this connection.

Your spirit guides know your mission in life and will help you. They have a larger perspective and know what will help you and what will not. I know from experience that our guides will help out in many areas of our lives, such as our jobs, our health, or a possible accident. However, they often will not help when we need to figure something out for ourselves. For instance, it is often difficult to find out about our future. The reason why is because they do not want to interfere with lessons that we need to learn.

In many respects, we are helpless without our spirit guides. If you look at other people's lives and wonder why they have had a successful life, it can be attributed to their guides. No one succeeds in life without help from the other side. Normally, people do not even realize they are receiving help. In a general sense, people are oblivious to the interaction that takes place between us and our spirit guides. As people become more spiritually aware, they begin to recognize this interaction. Many Christians call this the *grace of God.*

Relying on ourselves – our egos – puts us at the mercy of the physical world. To become more powerful, more conscious, and more spiritually aware, we must connect with our spirit guides. They know what we need even more than we do. Our consciousness is very limited on this physical plane. Souls on the Other Side are more spiritually aware. More than that, it is their mission to give us guidance. All we have to do is pay attention.

Nobody is alone and unable to communicate with their guides. In fact, everyone is constantly influenced by the Other Side. So, instead of ignoring this connection, work with it. Use your intuition and not your logical mind, and pay attention to details. Intuitively *feel* your way through life.

Instead of living with thoughts, live with feelings. This is how we connect with our guides. These feelings can be very subtle, so it requires paying attention. Do not think the room is empty just because you are alone. Think in terms of interaction between yourself and your guides.

* * * * *

Feelings are often not practical or logical, and they can lead you in new directions. Some people think intuition is a slippery slope toward irresponsibility and unreliability. However, it is actually the road to spirituality. Following your heart is the one path you can trust.

Some of you may be wondering, how can I live by feelings – the heart – when I have been conditioned to live by logic – the mind? The better question is, do I want to become a more spiritual being?

In many respects, living by feelings is what most women do already. They live by feelings and intuition. It is said that love is blind. Most mothers do not judge their children. They love their children with their hearts, not their minds. They love unconditionally. Unconditional love comes from the inner self, the soul.

We have different types of intelligence, although science has yet to discover this. Our brain is only one type of intelligence that we have. This is why people like Forrest Gump (in the movie) can exhibit incredible spiritual qualities and common sense.

Our intuitions are another form of intelligence. In fact, intuition is the highest form of intelligence because it is a direct connection to the soul and spirit guides. Thus, by feeling, we can be guided by a supra-intelligence, which knows *everything*.

When Jesus said, "Of myself, I can do nothing," he was talking about the supra intelligence, the connection to our guides and higher self. He was aware that he was not alone, and he felt connected to the Other Side. Whereas we may not have the same ability to tap into this intelligence as Jesus was able to do, we can use it to guide our lives. Until we reach his level of awareness, we can use our connection to our spirit guides.

We can be like Jesus. We can walk with the awareness that we are not alone. Yes, Jesus was more aware of how to use this connection, but his degree of awareness was simply a matter of spiritual evolvement.

The connection to the Other Side comes from listening to the heart – by *feeling*. That is why Jesus was such a compassionate and loving man. It is said, that to know him was to love him. Instead of using his ego for guidance, he used his heart.

When we give up our egos and trust our hearts, a transformation occurs in our lives. The future no longer seems important. Other people's judgments no longer seem significant. Our lives take on a whole new meaning. It is the details of the moment that now matter the most to us.

The Other Side is influencing our lives, so we should pay attention. How can you perceive this influence? I believe that our guides are looking out for our best interests and that it is up to us to pay attention to their advice.

I have three rules for tapping into the Other Side. First, *trust* that your life is perfect, and that the world is divinely ordered. Second, *follow* your heart using your intuition (spirit led). Third, pay attention to the details in your life and listen to your guides. Using these guidelines, I have become very closely connected to the Other Side.

From rules such as these, you can give up decision-making to a certain degree. Yes, we have to make decisions and live our lives. However, with these rules, life takes on a new dimension. Decisions now have to *feel* right, as do our plans. I no longer do anything without the Universe's blessing.

Follow what *excites* you. That excitement and passion comes directly from your heart and soul. Live each day, adhering to the call of your intuition. You do not have to plan your life alone. You can let the Other Side help. Put the burden on them.

The key to living a harmonious life is paying attention to *today* and not worrying about tomorrow. Magically, as we begin to notice the details in our life, we stop thinking about tomorrow. The future becomes less important because we have our attention on today.

* * * * *

When unusual or traumatic events happen in your life, ask yourself why, and search for the answers. Stop and find the clues. These are the opportunities to manifest the life you came to live. These are the times when your guides are signaling your purpose in life, or at the very least, changes that need to be made to manifest that purpose.

For example, a crisis at work. This can be a sign that it is time to move on to a new job. Or it can be a lesson that you are working on in this lifetime. What is the crisis? How did it manifest? What is it trying to tell you? The key is not to get upset, but to get curious. You manifested the crisis, and you did it for a reason. What reason?

This is a different way to perceive life. When we begin to understand that we are here to learn specific lessons that pertain specifically to our self, then our awareness begins to expand. We begin to look at things from a different perspective. We begin to acknowledge that true reality exists on the spiritual plane, and that we are here on the physical plane simply to learn and evolve our soul.

As I have stated repeatedly, the physical plane is an illusion. Everything we feel or see is simply vibrating matter. In fact, it is possible to make something disappear by increasing its vibration. The physical dimension is a construct that scientists only have the vaguest notions about. The only thing that is not a construct of physical matter is the soul, which is pure energy. Our souls are literally connected to the Other Side. In fact, only a fragment of one's soul is actually here on this physical plane. The greater part of our soul remains on the Other Side, which is our true home.

To feel the connection to the Other Side, realize that you are connected to it. This is not as difficult as it sounds. The key is the details of your life. As you begin to notice the details, you become aware that there is a higher power involved in your life. Suddenly, you will have more coincidences. For instance, when you need something, it appears.

I literally put my life into the hands of those beings on the Other Side. Each day, I expect them to take care of me. I *expect* my day to be designed in advance and to go according to the higher plan. All I have to do is get up in the morning, feel my emotions, and follow my excitement. If the day does not go well, I look at the details for clues as to why it did not go harmoniously – I become curious.

To make a connection with your guides, be aware of the details in your life and pay attention to guidance. Have one foot in this world and one foot on the spiritual plane. The more aware of the spiritual plane we become, the more spiritual we become, and the more intuitive we become. We become spiritual beings not by being alone in our heads, but by being connected to the Other Side.

CHAPTER EIGHT

We Learn By Experience

Every experience is a doorway to our growth. It does not matter if an experience is positive or negative because all experiences lead to the same outcome: growth. For this reason, all experiences are valid.

If you are experiencing something in your life, there is a reason. It is not always apparent, but a reason exists. Life is confusing because we often do not understand why we are experiencing something. What is really happening is often camouflaged and hidden from our perceptions.

We incarnate to learn lessons that are provided by our experiences. When we incarnate, we purposely put ourselves in a state of amnesia. We do this so that we can learn from a fresh slate. Generally, the lessons we are learning we have experienced before and have failed to learn. In Michael Newton's book, *Journey of Souls*, it was stated that we generally fail to learn a lesson the first time we try. Often it requires multiple incarnations to learn the same lesson.

We are the sum of all of our experiences, over many lifetimes. Thus, there is meaning in every experience we have. We may not perceive the meaning, but it is there, nonetheless. Our souls are eternal, and we are affected by every experience we encounter.

Stop reading and reflect back on yesterday. Did you judge someone's behavior or a choice they made? Think carefully. Did you judge someone's behavior as less than ideal?

You may ask, what does judging someone's behavior have to do with the topic of this chapter – Learning by Experience? Our experiences are not only physical. In fact, most of our experiences are mental. Likewise, our experiences are what we take with us when we leave this life, and these are our mental thoughts and beliefs. How we mentally react to the world around us becomes a part of our soul.

Most people live in their minds, constantly judging the world around them. Thus, thoughts are experiences, too. Thoughts have energy. How we think creates our future, not just this lifetime but other ones as well.

Thought, more than anything else, is the precursor to experience because we create our experiences by what we think and believe. This is why nothing happens by accident. Everything happens according to our beliefs. The mind is the builder.

Incredibly, God has the ability to act like a giant computer, compiling everyone's beliefs and making them work together in perfect harmony. If we had an inkling of the complexity that controls every action on the planet, we would be amazed. There is no randomness.

How can there be no randomness? The answer is that everything is *one*. We think in terms of separation when actually there is no separation. An analogy can be made to the cells in our body. Each cell is alive and has a consciousness of its own. However, it is also connected and interrelated to all of the other cells in your body. If we feel fear, all of our cells feel fear.

In the same way that all of the cells in our body are related and connected, everything in the universe is related and connected. This relatedness and interaction prevents randomness. In effect, all experiences are reactions to the interaction of consciousness. Thus, how we react to the world creates our experiences.

God is a controlling force in the universe. God is the consciousness of All That Is. This consciousness permeates *everything* and is what causes the interrelation and interaction. We are all one because we are all *God*. In effect, there is no separation between anything.

God is not a being. God is. What does this mean? Let us put it this way, if God is everything and thus infinite, how can we define God as a being? God can manifest as a point of consciousness, such as ourselves manifested as souls. However, that point of consciousness will not encompass the *entirety* of God. We are manifestations of God as points of consciousness, but we are not the entirety of God. Stated another way, we are fragments of God.

The equality among souls is the basis for non-judgment on the higher planes. The higher etheric planes are where we came from and where we return after this incarnation is over. Those who have NDEs remember it as home and often do not want to return their body after they have felt the love and harmony that exists on the higher planes.

The harmony and love that exist on the higher planes create a nirvana-like environment that is not conducive to experiencing lessons that can evolve the soul. This is why we incarnate on the physical plane. In other words, we desire experiences that can evolve the soul. The irony is that these experiences, which we have come to learn during this lifetime, are not always fun. However, they are challenging. And there's the reward: we want a challenge.

When we planned this life, we chose how challenging it would be. If your life is extremely challenging, that was a choice you made before you arrived. My niece recently had a baby. When I did the child's natal horoscope, I told my niece she had a fantastic horoscope, and I explained why. However, when I was done, I told her that when someone chooses a strong horoscope, they usually do that in tandem with a challenging life so that the horoscope can help them succeed.

Some souls are quite content to have a lifetime where they have one career job, one wife, two kids, and a dog. Basically, a routine life. However, other souls are much more ambitious, and want an adventure. These are the souls who choose challenges, and want an array of diverse experiences to fill their cup to the brim. When they get back home, they want a story to tell that is not boring.

There is risk in choosing a challenging life. What risk? Getting off the path of what you came to learn. The temptations of the world or the slippery slope of the ego's control of your life, can lead you astray. To be succinct, you can make a mess of your life quite easily (how many people do you know who fit that description?). This is why most people live boring lives and grow their soul very slowly. Those who live in the fast lane are taking risks.

After this incarnation, when we arrive back home to our particular place on the higher planes, God will not judge us. However, the concept of judgment at death is valid. This is why it is so ingrained in us. At death, we do indeed look back on our lives in great detail, starting with a life review. The results of these life reviews will have a great bearing on our souls. One reason people believe God is a being is because highly evolved souls help us understand our recent lifetimes and help us plan our next ones. Although these beings do not necessarily judge us, they do point out how we fared, and they recommend future experiences to evolve the soul.

Those who chose challenging lives and made a mess of it, often get to repeat the challenge. This is another reason many souls prefer to take it slowly. Once you get in the fast lane, it's hard to slow down. It's like joining the Marines. Once you join, you are always a Marine.

So, when you are doing a life review, and you are one of those souls who likes challenges, it's not likely that you are going to regress. You're not going to say, I want a career job this time and one wife!

Most of us have incarnated so many times that this life review encounter with advanced souls is branded into our consciousness. We have deep memories of conversing with souls much more advanced than ourselves. This memory manifests as a belief that these advanced souls are God, and will judge us when we die. On a subconscious level, we know we must meet with them again when we die. In essence, everyone gets a report card for this lifetime. The good news is that everyone passes. The bad news is that our karma catches up to us and forces us to live challenging lives.

Only a small percentage of people are consciously aware that there is nothing to fear at death and that our souls return to the higher planes. For the vast majority of people, however, the concept of death produces fear. The subconscious is aware that something happens after death. These memories are strong and create a deep sense of fear because we sense a responsibility. We sense that how we live and the decisions we make affect our future. And guess what? They do!

Before we are born into our bodies, we carefully plan our lives. We know in advance the possibilities. We determine how we will look, our personalities, and intelligence. We choose our parents, potential friends and jobs, potential experiences with other people, our spirit guides, and the purposes of our incarnations. The details that go into planning our lives are meticulous.

What appears to be random in our lives, we have already set into motion before birth. Everyone comes into the world with a blueprint, which is our life plan. These blueprints include our natal horoscope (the locations of the planets when we took our first breaths), the reasons we incarnated, our guides, our agreements with other souls, and many other factors. These are some of the forces that impinge on our lives. As you can see, our lives are much more planned and controlled than we generally perceive.

The concept of free will is more limited than generally understood. For instance, if an experience is not our blueprint, then we are not going to have it. What we do have in life is the ability to make choices. For instance, we can choose a job, where to take a vacation, and what we're going to have for dinner. Thus, we can make choices to a certain extent, but our blueprints limit our experiences. For instance, we will choose only those jobs or spouses that match our blueprints.

Our soul knows why we came and what we need to learn during our lives. We can stray to a certain extent, but basically, we decide our lives before we are born. Yes, we can break agreements, such as an agreement to marry a certain person, but we cannot stray very far outside of our blueprints. All of our experiences are potentials that we were aware of at birth. Nothing can happen to us in this life that we did not agree to.

Thus, all is perfection, and there is no randomness. If someone is sexually abused, that person realized before birth it could happen, and accepted that potential outcome. We know before birth the kind of people we will interact with and the *potential* experiences we might have. We agree to expose ourselves to these experiences in order to learn what our souls need.

We have the potential to succeed or fail in our life goals, and nobody is doomed to failure. Moreover, all of the potential outcomes are known in advance. The outcome we prefer, which is what we want before we incarnate, is always a possibility. However, life does not always go according to our plans – our preferred outcomes. And many of us fail to learn our lessons. Alas, that does not matter, since time does not exist. We can always learn the lesson on attempt number two, three, four, and on and on.

As souls, few of us are highly advanced, or we would not be here. We are using this negative environment to evolve and grow spiritually. We desire to experience negativity in order to evolve. For, once we evolve upward, we may never again get the opportunity again. In other words, being Bonnie Parker or Clyde Barrow – the famous bank robbers – was not necessarily a bad thing. Learning through negative experiences is something we all do by design.

* * * * *

Most people do not realize how powerful they are. Did you know that nothing can happen to you unless your soul wants it to, and that you get exactly what you need? We individually create our own reality – all of it.

Everyone's soul is vibrating at a certain frequency. Moreover, our own particular frequency creates our interactions with other people. Have you wondered why you seem to have a connection with some people and not others? It is energy. We all have an aura, which is an energy field that emanates from the soul. Other people can feel it on a subconscious level. Our vibrations are what attracts us to each other. Give scientists a few decades, and they will be able to measure everyone's frequency and vibration rate.

In the future (in our lifetime), doctors will treat people *before* they become sick by viewing their auras and rebalancing their energy fields. Most people will rarely get sick because they will have easy access to healers who can *prevent* illness. There will also be machines that use sound or color to balance the aura. These machines will be used to treat illness and prevent illness. The days of illness and big pharma are almost over.

Our auras and vibrations are constantly changing. Let me give an example. Edgar Cayce could see people's auras. He could tell when they were angry because their auras would become tinged with red. The angrier they became, the redder the hue. When people became absolutely livid, he told them to come back after they had settled down. He said this gently and with love. "Please come back after you have calmed down."

Our auras and vibrations have a huge impact on our experiences. When we interact with people, our auras and vibrations adjust to the situations we are in. Each of us is a dazzling rainbow of energy that is constantly in flux. And our thoughts and beliefs determine our constantly changing auras.

Life happens something like this: we react to our environments by our beliefs. Our reactions create our emotions. Our emotions trigger our thoughts. Our thoughts release energy and cause our auras to fluctuate into radiant colors.

Only a rare person today has the benefit of being able to see an aura, although this is changing as we transition into the fourth dimension. Most people can *feel* other people's auras – energy fields – and respond subconsciously. Have you ever met someone you instantly felt attracted to or repulsed by? Did you wonder where that feeling came from? You were responding to the person's energy field.

I remember how sensitive my cat was to other people's energy. She would go to the door if the person was a cat lover, or run under the bed if it was a cat hater. And she would know before they even knocked on the door!

My point is this: your energy field has a huge impact on the experiences you have. More importantly, you have control over that energy field by the beliefs you hold. Previously, I wrote about the frequency of love, thereby living from a place of neutrality and unconditional love. That is one example of how to change your energy field.

* * * * *

Each life (many of us have lived more than a thousand) is similar to a school grade level. In fact, many sources on the higher planes who channel information to us on Earth, refer to Earth as a school. They say that incarnating is much like a typical school system in which we advance one grade level at a time. We either stay at the same grade level, or we advance as we learn our lessons. There is a possibility of regressing, but this is extremely rare.

To use another school analogy, algebra is generally not taught to second graders. Children are taught what they are ready for, such as how to read. This is how reincarnation works. We are all exposed to what we need. Each and every experience we have directly correlates to what we need. It may not always appear this way, but it is true.

We are all receiving the experiences we require for our growth. What another person requires is not for us to judge. All is perfection in the eyes of God. To look upon another person as imperfect is to deny their divinity. And, as I mentioned before, the law of co-resonance will lower your frequency when you deny the divine in another. Why? Because if you don't believe that they are divine, then you must not believe that you are divine either. Basically, you are denying that your soul exists or that God exists. This naiveté keeps your frequency from rising.

The key to spiritual growth and spiritual awakening is being aware that everyone is experiencing what they need. Our role is not to wake up others to their follies, but to allow them their experiences and to focus on waking up ourselves.

There is no time limit for our spiritual awakening. In fact, there is no such thing as time, except here in the illusion of the physical plane. The time it takes to awaken is inconsequential. If someone appears to be failing in life, it very well could be what that person needs most.

Today, in the New Age movement, it is widely accepted that spiritual enlightenment is the goal of life. This is true to a certain extent, but how we decide to live our lives is each person's choice. Moreover, there is no right or wrong way to achieve enlightenment. My point is that *all* experiences lead to the same outcome: enlightenment. Growth will happen to nearly everyone (99.9%) regardless of our choices.

Have you heard the expression that everyone is at a different spiritual level? This is indeed the case. Nearly everyone steadily advances one spiritual level at a time, until they reach the top: enlightenment, which is an awareness of God. That is the meaning of life.

Each of our lives is a blip of experience in the overall knowledge of the soul. So, do not take life too seriously. Each life is meant to offer us new lessons through which we can grow. No life is wasted, and no experience is wasted. We use it all.

Unconditional love is allowing other people to be themselves, allowing them to choose their experiences without judgment, and loving them no matter what their behavior. Unconditional love is a reflection of spiritual awareness. Most people are not aware enough to accept other people's choices. The result is a very judgmental society. For love to flow on this planet, we have to recognize that everyone is experiencing what they need. We need to stop questioning other people's choices.

Nothing happens to anyone that is not supposed to happen. Everything happens because it is needed for the soul's growth. Thus, we do not need to try to save anyone. Our role as a spiritually awakened person is to set an example and to allow others to live as they wish without condemning them.

Most of these concepts must be learned through experience. For instance, when we manipulate someone into living as *we* want them to live, the outcome teaches us a valuable lesson. The karma from such an experience may lead us to be manipulated in the future, either in this lifetime or another. Eventually, we learn to allow people to make their own choices.

Once we have advanced spiritually to the point where we are ready to love unconditionally, new experiences and new lessons are possible. Once we are able to love people unconditionally, nothing they do or say diminishes that feeling. Experiences such as this teach us about unconditional love.

When we understand that everyone's life is perfect and they are trying as hard as they can, we will support their efforts. When we decide to support someone, no matter what their choices, we are able to love them unconditionally. When people realize we love them unconditionally, they respond in a like manner. It is a natural response. Love creates love.

One of the laws of the universe is that when we force our will upon others, we create karma for ourselves. This means we cannot manipulate others without karmic ramifications. Most of the lessons we are learning revolve around breaking this law. Every thought and action we do is noted and saved in the Akashic records – God's record book. Each lifetime is stored as a lifeprint. These records reveal how we have created and resolved our karma. They are the history of our souls. Thus, we must always resolve the karma we create. This is why every soul is different. Everyone creates their own unique karma, and everyone must live their own unique lives to resolve their karma.

What does it mean to manipulate another? It means that we are denying that person's sovereignty, and we are impinging on their choices. Once we understand this – through our life experiences – that is when we begin to allow people to make their own choices. Instead of thinking we know what is best for others, we realize they are quite capable of living their own lives. This is when we begin creating love and having experiences that revolve around unconditional love.

* * * * *

One way to start becoming spiritual is to realize that everyone is trying as hard as they can. Thus, when someone pulls out in front of you when you are driving, try not to become upset. Instead, send a loving mental request for that person to be more careful next time. Remember, thoughts are real. If you get upset, then on a subconscious level, the driver will perceive this to be judgment. From this perception, the driver will likely continue to drive haphazardly.

We all feel energy from other people subconsciously. We are constantly bombarded by a stream of other people's thoughts. In effect, we are constantly being tested, and the Universe (God) is monitoring how we react. At all times, God wants to know where we are spiritually. Thus, our spirituality – our beliefs – dictate our experiences.

To become spiritual, we must learn to love unconditionally. That is the one lesson we are all here to learn, and we learn it through our experiences. We have to learn not to manipulate people and not to judge people. This cannot be learned in one lifetime, but requires many, and one experience at a time. All of our experiences are directed with this goal in mind.

Chapter Nine

Spiritual Knowledge

To be self-reliant and self-empowered, we need knowledge. Not just any kind of knowledge, but spiritual knowledge. This is the knowledge that provides spiritual wisdom. And the more spiritual knowledge we possess, the more wisdom we will have.

What kind of wisdom? The ability to make decisions. The ability to act. If you can respond with love to any situation, you are self-empowered. In the New Age movement, we call this being in your power, or "holding" your power. This is the power of your soul, the power of your sovereignty. Let me give a few examples.

Say you are in line at a store to purchase something. A stranger decides to crowd in front of you. How do you react? Do you get upset? Do you ask if you can have your place back?

The answer is that you love. You smile and take a step back, giving room. Anyone who recklessly forces his or her will upon others needs tons of love. What is wanted by the interloper is a reaction. Why? They are frustrated and unhappy, and they want you to be, too.

When we are wise, we do not let anyone upset us. Instead, we remain calm and "hold" our power. Spiritual wisdom is how to hold that power. In the above example, the person obviously was not spiritually aware and was crying out for help. He knew in his heart he was equal to everyone, but no one would treat him as their equal. Instead, people looked at him with judgmental eyes. The result is he acted out his frustration and crowded into line. A person can take only so much judgment before acting out.

Another example: Say that you are Black, and you decide to start a business. The business you want requires a large loan, but that shouldn't be a problem because you have enough equity in your house for collateral to offset the risk, and you have excellent credit. You know that banks make loans like this all the time.

The first bank is blatantly discriminatory. You are barely asked any questions and told they do not make loans like this. You know they do, but you hold your anger and walk out the door. The next bank asks many more questions, but you can tell they do not want your business. The third bank is even worse. The loan officer looks over the documents, makes a squeamish face, and shakes his head.

What do you do? You realize that the people are discriminating because that is all they know. It is futile to try to change their behavior, and pointless to get upset. In such a situation, all we can do is smile and walk out the door. Moreover, thank the loan officer for his time. Then go to the next bank, or try again in six months with the same banks that turned you down.

Everything has a purpose. If there is discrimination, there is a purpose for it. People who are discriminating do not know any better. However, lessons are being learned. Any form of prejudice or discrimination comes from ignorance. Acknowledge the ignorance, but do not become upset. Just see it. Allow the Universe (God) to find a way to rectify the situation. If you are supposed to get the loan, it will happen.

Wisdom manifests when we have spiritual knowledge. Knowing why things occur, such as recognizing discrimination, can be very empowering. Conversely, becoming upset and not recognizing a lack of awareness in another person reduces our power and self-reliance.

With spiritual wisdom, we can be treated unfairly, yet accept the experience with equanimity. With wisdom, we perceive someone's lack of spiritual awareness and react accordingly. With wisdom, we can smile in the face of adversity with a calm sense of *knowing*. That, my friend, is empowerment.

When we come to realize that everything is a perfect manifestation of God, nothing upsets us. We are empowered. We see the world from a new perspective. We see life as a God-given right to live as we choose. We see that our own lives are just as valid as those of others, and vice versa. To have this kind of spiritual awareness requires obtaining spiritual knowledge. In other words, we have to learn how God works. We have to take a spiritual path.

The question arises, is it worth it to spend time searching for spiritual knowledge? I submit that life becomes easier and more satisfying with spiritual awareness. People and events no longer affect you negatively. Surely, this is worth obtaining.

Let me give another example. Once when Gandhi was arrested for instigating a rebellion in India, he was taken to prison. When he was given a mop and told to clean a latrine, he smiled, nodded, and said to the guard, "Thank you." Then he proceeded to enjoy himself while cleaning the latrine. He had absolutely no frustration or bitterness.

Gandhi was empowered because he was spiritually aware. He knew it was only a matter of time before the British would go home. He understood that India had allowed the

British to assume control of the country and he was not bitter. He also was aware that all he needed to do to create change was to calmly believe it. If he could get enough other people to believe, it would come to pass.

No country or individual is powerless. Quite the opposite. In fact, a country receives exactly what it believes, just as individuals receive exactly what they believe. Thus, Gandhi was changing the hearts of his people more than he was the resolve of the British. Gandhi knew this, and he knew his mission was to teach his people, so he felt no antagonism toward the British.

Not all of us need to be like Gandhi or a leader. Do not confuse Gandhi's quest for independence as an example of how to live your own life. For most of us, it is only ourselves with whom we need to be concerned. To create positive change, the best way is to change yourself, not to try to change others.

Gandhi was self-empowered because he had spiritual wisdom. He could face any situation that confronted him. He had courage and resolve. He knew life is an illusion and that real power is hidden. He was humble because he knew there is a power greater than ourselves, a power directly connected with our lives and that this power can be tapped, which he did.

Gandhi was doing what came naturally to him. He was a teacher. It just so happened his class was the entire world. Gandhi realized that God exists in each of us. He also realized God is in charge, and that the plan of humanity is under God's direction. Yes, humanity has a big influence on the direction, but it is God's grand plan. Once we realize this, it is difficult not to want to serve humanity.

Gandhi offered selfless service to humanity. He gave his life to help others. He was not concerned with his own ego. He sacrificed his personal pursuits in order to serve humanity, and he did it on a grand scale. Yet Gandhi was but a reflection of the millions of people who give selfless service to humanity every day.

Once we realize that our lives are part of God's grand plan, it is difficult not to want to help. We begin to think about how we can help. What should we do to help humanity? Should we ignore humanity's cry for help or do what we can? Once we are spiritually aware, it is compelling to do our share.

Most of us have small, bit parts. All we have to do is learn to love ourselves and to love others. When we can do that, we are able to spread love in untold ways. Currently, society is enveloped in darkness, although that is changing as more people are exposed to metaphysical and spiritual knowledge. To balance this darkness, we can spread love and act as examples. This has the effect of transforming darkness into light.

* * * * *

Spiritual knowledge is the key to spiritual awareness. As more and more people become exposed to spiritual knowledge and metaphysical wisdom, the global population's awareness will expand. People will begin to realize they are God and that so is everyone else. This awe-inspiring change is near fruition. Once we achieve critical mass, society will experience a complete transformation. Everything from medicine to politics to relationships will completely change.

The more spiritually aware we are, the more we are empowered. The ultimate example was Jesus. He was at peace because he was enlightened. He understood there was nothing to fear, that he and God were one, and that so is everything else. Jesus' level of awareness was so high that nothing affected his being. We also can attain that degree of peace, although not necessarily in this lifetime.

Currently, spiritual awareness is not highly valued by society. This is mainly because our lives generally do not require spiritual awareness in a competitive world. On the contrary, the more spiritually asleep we are, the more we fit in. Conversely, the more spiritually aware we are, the more eccentric and strange we appear.

This is, however, about to change. In the near future, spiritual awareness will become highly valued. People will realize that the spiritual values that Newagers hold are indeed important, such as the following:

- We are God, and so is everyone and everything else.
- Everyone's life is perfect.
- Everyone creates their own reality by their beliefs.
- There are no accidents.
- Life is an illusion.
- Reincarnation is a reality.
- Spirituality is a personal matter.

Grasping these spiritual concepts requires many incarnations. Our level of spiritual development determines our spiritual awareness and how well we grasp them. A young soul, who has only incarnated a few times, may not grasp any of these concepts, whereas an old soul may grasp them all.

What is spiritual awareness? It is knowledge of reality. For instance, when someone attacks you verbally, do you become angry? Such a response comes from a lack of awareness. An enlightened person recognizes that any attack is a call for love, a cry for help. Thus, the correct response is either no response, or a response of compassion. Verbal attackers expect a reaction, a confirmation that you do not love them. What they really want is proof that unconditional love does not exist.

When you know who you are (God) and why you are here, you do not feel the need to defend yourself. You no longer get upset or anxious when others question your choices. No explanation is necessary, only your example.

Knowing who you are and why you are on Earth provides you with spiritual knowledge. Such knowledge provides you with wisdom: the ability to make decisions in the face of societal pressures. Wisdom, when you truly define the word, is the ability to direct your own life. Spiritual awareness gives you the ability to be at peace and the power to maintain that peace.

Your Soul Explained

CHAPTER TEN

What Is Evil?

We are told from birth there is right and wrong, good and bad. However, evil is categorized on a far worse, demonic level. The very word *evil* is associated with the devil, a vile, treacherous being believed to exist apart from God, a being whose very nature is considered the epitome of evil.

Today, the belief in evil prevents us from loving each other and is the basis of judgment, as well as the basis for the duality that keeps us separate: good guys versus bad guys. Evil is considered dangerous, wrong, vile, and to be avoided. At a young age, we are conditioned to believe that evil is the worst thing on Earth. No specific definition is given, just the warning that it exists and to avoid it.

What do people label evil? Anything that upsets them. For instance, Dr. Jack Kevorkian, one of the first proponents of euthanasia, is considered evil by many, yet a savior by others. People define evil based on their beliefs, but their interpretative power is precarious.

No clear distinction is made when one crosses the line from being bad to being evil. We can be bad and still not be evil. For instance, many white-collar criminals are not considered evil, although they usually are labeled as bad. Even a murderer may not be labeled evil. It depends on the circumstances.

Evil does exist, just not in the way most people perceive it. Evil is the manifestation of negative energy, the absence of harmony or positive energy. Both negative and positive energy are valid experiences. Both lead to the same outcome: enlightenment.

Not all of our lessons can be learned in a harmonious way. Under these circumstances, we use negative energy. This is why evil is *live* spelled backwards. People who use negative energy are in a sense, living backwards. In the end, their negative experiences (which we all have) will add to their soul development. They will use the negative experiences to "turn around" and learn to live in harmony.

Evil (negative experience) is not separate from God. All experiences are perfect manifestations of God. You may not want to hear this. You may be wondering if you should even be reading this. That is how entrenched the belief in the devil (the so-called root of evil) is.

Society is often quick to judge something as evil when, in fact, it is not even negative energy. For example, astrology is often judged as being occult, and that anyone using astrology is dealing with evil forces. Many people will not even investigate the authenticity of astrology, because of its association with the occult. Ironically, astrology will soon be proven scientifically to be real.

Then, there is the double standard of good and evil. For instance, many Catholic Priests molested boys, but the Vatican never deemed them evil. Yet, they never hesitate to label abortion or pornography as evil. Hypocrisy is common today in the judgment of what is evil. We often request a light sentence for a friend, and a harsh sentence for a stranger who is deemed evil.

Have you wondered why mothers come to the defense of their children? They usually will provide love and understanding, no matter what the charge. Do you think God is any different? Do you think God becomes upset with people by their behavior? If you fear God is going to be upset with you when you arrive in heaven, you are in for a pleasant surprise. It does not matter what you do in life; God will welcome you with love and compassion. After all, God knew in advance what you were going to do anyway.

God knows we are undeveloped souls. We were created to learn from our mistakes and all of our experiences. God simply points us to the next lifetime and the next set of lessons. God helps us along. God has infinite patience.

God is *us*. Our identity is an illusion. We think we are separate from God. In actuality, we are an idea of God. Our soul is simply the manifestation of an idea of God. In essence, we are a part of God. God simply took a piece of its consciousness and released it. God cannot create without creating from itself. This is why there is no separation between God and anything.

So, when you point your finger and say that is evil, you are denying God's existence. But, if you say that is some ugly, negative energy, you will likely be correct. That is the darkness on the planet that we are here to remove. It will not be removed by judgment, but by shining our light (unconditional love) on it. Thus, light removes darkness and not judgment. Light restores harmony.

* * * * *

One of the most interesting facets of God is the laws. Understanding God's laws makes it easier to find our way through life. Moreover, we can use these laws to understand how God controls the grand plan, and the interconnection of all life.

One law is not to infringe our will upon another. Think about what that says. It implies that we should be humble and compassionate and in accord with all other consciousness. It also implies that if we force our wills upon others, we create karma for ourselves. This is one of the reasons to be leery of having too much self-interest. Self-interest is something that must come into accordance with this law. If we are too egotistical and ambitious, we are bound to have too much self-interest. The result is we likely will infringe our will upon others.

Understand that the karma we build has to be paid back. That is another law. Whenever we force our wills upon others, we create karma. For instance, if you harm someone or change someone's destiny, this creates karma for yourself. Karma is a concept that implies retribution of some kind. Thus, whenever we create karma, it must be resolved in some way. Often, our lives are spent resolving our karma from past lives. Thus, when you see a homeless person, it is possible that he or she forced someone into poverty in another life and is now resolving his or her karma.

Karma teaches us to respect others. All of us are creators, and we have incredible creative powers. Unless we learn to create with responsibility, we will make mistakes that affect others. For instance, as we evolve, we eventually attain the power to create almost instantly. The moment we think of our intended creation, it happens. This is called manifesting. Karma teaches us how to manifest responsibly.

Karma is not a black-and-white issue. For instance, after this life, you will do a life review and analyze the karma you created. The analysis will determine what karma you must resolve. This determination is done by you with the help of advanced souls.

In many respects, the karma created during a lifetime is easy to grasp afterward. We generally can see where we made mistakes in forcing our wills upon others. Understand that your entire soul, which is much more than you currently realize, is doing the analyzing.

No matter how intense the karma you create, the result is only additional learning experiences to resolve. Even a person such as Charles Manson will be allowed to resolve his karma. From this perspective, how evil is he? And if Charles Manson is not an evil person, who is?

The end result of a soul like Charles Manson is that he will evolve just like you and me. Is there anything positive from Manson's life? I think so. Yes, he murdered several people, but what about the pain and suffering he prevented? Think of the many people who recognized the mistake Manson committed and did not repeat it, such as by joining a cult.

Charles Manson was a very confused person, most likely insane. He does not fit in society. His striking back at society is known by millions. How many people have considered striking back at society yet realized the futility because of Manson's example? I submit that his life has had some positive effects. I cannot think of one instance of another Manson. No one has repeated his act. In essence, he showed us what not to do.

What about other bad guys, such as rapists and murderers? What is their redeeming value? As stated earlier, all experiences are perfect manifestations of God. Yet, how can we explain the bad guys? First, is it possible you were a rapist or a murderer in another life? The answer is probably yes. Thus, evil in one lifetime does not always lead to evil in another. Identifying a person as evil is generally an inaccurate observation because we are only seeing a fragment of the soul and not its entirety.

We commit negative acts in order to learn and evolve. Everyone has done it in one lifetime or another. If there is such a thing as evil, then we all have been evil. God does use a boundary of negativity that must not be crossed, but that boundary is extraordinarily high and cannot be crossed in a single lifetime. Rarely does God – actually, very wise souls who act as surrogates – decide that a soul is not redeemable.

The next question that arises is why? Why does God allow such heinous acts? The answer is simple: God desires to evolve, and the best way is to experience the infinite: *all* experiences. The physical plane is an environment that allows the infinite to be experienced, both positive and negative.

Heinous acts occur from our limited awareness and the illusion of the physical plane. We, here on Earth, create these acts together. No one behaves in isolation. Any idea that pops into someone's head is the result of the mass consciousness. If a person chooses to rape or murder, it is because society had considered these as options. These are ideas society as a whole thinks and, thus, creates.

If O.J. Simpson did murder his wife, he thought about it beforehand. First, the idea of murder popped into his head as an option. Then, the idea intensified. Where did the idea come from? How many people think of killing other people? Why is the idea of murder so prevalent? Is this idea a manifestation of society's current spiritual consciousness? I submit that it is. In other words, O.J. did not act alone. We, as a society, are accomplices.

The mass consciousness exists, yet as a society, we have not considered such a concept. As a society, we are not yet ready to accept this because it will change everything. For one thing, we will recognize that, as a society, we are all responsible for Nicole Simpson's death and all of the other murders that are taking place on a daily basis.

Society today believes we are only responsible for our own actions. The concept of a mass consciousness will turn everything upside down. No longer will we judge people and assign blame. The fact is we are constantly bombarded by stimuli, which is the result of the mass consciousness. Each of us adds to the planet's mass consciousness, and each of us is affected by it. Nobody lives in isolation.

Today, we live in a very negative environment, and most people are adding to that negativity. Everyone is responsible for the negativity, because everyone is a part of the mass consciousness. Once enough people begin living positive lifestyles and add to the harmony on the planet, the mass consciousness will change, and our experiences will change.

How we think and believe as a whole creates the experiences of life. Every decision we make is made within the context of the current mass consciousness. Thus, if O.J. killed his wife, then we, as a group, pushed him to do it. We gave him that option. He did not act in isolation. No one does.

Each of us reacts to the stimuli in our lives. Society – the mass consciousness – creates the stimuli, and we react depending on the life lessons we need to learn. There is no right or wrong. There is reaction. There are choices. We are all manifestations of God, reacting to our environment. It is not a moral play. It is not about good and evil. It is about experiencing and evolving.

Each of us attracts the experiences that happen to us. Everything happens in conjunction with the mass consciousness and soul lessons that need to be learned.

We tend to think that our conscious mind is in charge of our lives. In fact, the subconscious is in control and much more powerful. The subconscious understands our beliefs more clearly, as well as the beliefs of others.

* * * * *

It is said that Jesus did not protest or resist his arrest by the Sanhedrin. When Jesus was brought before the Sanhedrin council to answer charges that he was breaking their laws, he calmly answered their questions. He never proclaimed his innocence. He did not proclaim that they should free him.

Jesus' response to his arrest is my favorite story about his life. He lived his word. He did not resist evil. His response was to shine his light. He stood before the council and said, "Judge me, if that is what you want to do." He allowed them to do whatever they wished.

By not resisting, Jesus showed us that to change evil, we must transform it, and that we transform evil by shining our light. By giving his life, Jesus helped people see it is wrong to kill an innocent man. He also helped us realize it is better to transform evil than attempt to destroy it. That, in fact, it is impossible to destroy evil with evil. The only effect of attempting to destroy evil is the creation of more evil. The only effect of war is more war. The only effect of hatred is more hatred. The "troubles" in Northern Ireland or the Israeli / Palestinian conflict are perfect examples.

Today, society believes in the duality of right and wrong, good and evil. Society points to evil and wants to find ways to destroy it. This is futile.

Jesus said, "Love your enemies." And who are your enemies, if not evil people? In fact, it is an illusion that there are such things as enemies. The way to combat evil is to shine your light, to be an example of love. Germany and France fought a war and are now friends. The United States and

Japan fought a war and are now friends. Love your enemy, and they will no longer be your enemy.

Likewise, the more we forgive evil, the less it will manifest. The less we judge and condemn, the more love that will manifest. Evil is something that we create as a society, and it is something we can remove as a society. In fact, we are living in the end times of evil. The more love that manifests, the less evil that will exist.

I mentioned some of God's laws in this chapter. Another one is that what is true is *always* true. This is the law that will end wars and most of the dark energy (evil) on the planet. Why? Because we will use this law as the foundation for the next civilization. When someone claims something to be true, they will need to prove that it is always true.

If you can't prove something is always true, then it is an opinion, an idea. We won't base our laws, rules, and regulations on someone's opinion. We will use the truth instead. For instance, the following are always true:

- Everything is consciously connected.
- Everyone is a divine being.
- Everyone has a soul.
- Everyone has a blueprint.
- The core of our soul is love.
- The meaning of life is to expand our awareness of God.
- This planet is a school for souls.

Can you imagine what society would look like based on those truths? Get ready, because that's our future. Once the truth is released, there is no going back to ignorance. You can't unknow the truth.

CHAPTER ELEVEN

Fear Is from a Lack of Awareness

When I learned that fear and the truth cannot coexist, it was a surprise. I knew that fear could be alleviated through belief, but I did not realize that it could be eliminated by *knowing* the truth. The very existence of fear shows that we don't know the truth completely. We all know part of the truth, but once we know it completely, fear evaporates.

Jesus is a good example. So are the Buddha and other avatars who have walked on this planet. They had zero fear because they *knew* that they were God and that God is eternal and perfect. Moreover, on the spiritual planes where we exist as light beings, fear does not exist. So, fear is an illusion that we create on the physical plane. Fear is not real. It is an idea.

Now we know why the saying, *The Truth Shall Set You Free*, resonates with us. However, what we don't realize is that obtaining the truth is not easy. It takes effort and experience. We have to learn what the truth is. We have to obtain it.

Fear is our proof that we lack spiritual awareness and lack the truth. We can use that as a building block for steadily reducing our fears. And as we reduce our fears, we become more spiritually aware. That is our spiritual path.

* * * * *

All fear is based on what *might* happen. If we are each creating our reality – and we are – everything that happens is supposed to happen. So, why worry about what might be? There is always a reason for our experiences. It is something we need.

Many people believe fear controls us, but it does not. Beliefs control people, not fear. Fear is an emotion, the result of a belief. The basis of emotions is beliefs, not the other way around.

Fear is self-created from a lack of awareness. It is created from the belief that we are alone and separate from God. Do you think Jesus was afraid to be nailed to the cross? I believe he approached it with equanimity and accepted his fate without fear. He understood. He was aware.

The way to eliminate fear is to trust the Universe (God). If you are trusting that your life was perfectly planned and that only what you need can happen, then you can trust the outcome. However, to achieve this level of trust, you must become highly spiritually aware – you have to learn the truth.

* * * * *

In a dualistic system of belief, love and fear are opposites. Love is the positive aspect of the consciousness of God, and fear is the negative. Because many people live in fear, the negative aspect of consciousness has manifested to a high degree. Now you know why the world is such a scary place. Once we begin living more from love, the world will become a much more peaceful place.

Currently the world is enveloped by negative energy because of the widespread lack of spiritual awareness, which has created the confusion and fear predominant today. We have manifested a world based on power because of our preoccupation with fear.

When we fear lack, we seek to achieve abundance. That's why we have a world today based on power and materialism. Instead of loving each other, we compete over resources – who gets the nicest stuff. We seek achievement in order to reduce our fear.

From fear, comes the desire for self-interest. From self-interest, comes the desire for power over others. From the desire for power, comes the desire for control. This pretty much sums up society today. A thirst for power has created an elite class, the top 10% who own 90% of the wealth. This elite class manipulates and controls society. In many respects, they dictate how we live, adding to the fear we already have regarding our spiritual identities.

This sounds dour, but such is the state of humanity today. Thankfully, this is changing. As more people become spiritually aware, fear is diminishing. Fear is always about losing something, and those who are spiritually aware understand that they can only lose something that they do not need or want.

What is the result of a society consumed with fear? I contend that it has produced too much self-interest, which has led to a lack of humanity. The elite look out for themselves more than they look out for humanity. It is in their self-interest to look after their assets in order to maintain their wealth and power. Until society is concerned for all of mankind – peace, freedom, equality, compassion, caring – power will dominate love as the most coveted thing. When power is more coveted than love, something is terribly negative about a society. In fact, the very basis of our current society is negative: power. Note: I am not talking about self-empowerment, but exerting power over others in a controlling manner.

Amazingly, the basis of society – power – is the antithesis of love. Power may seem sexy, but it literally destroys love. It does this because power is closely associated with the ego, which is uncaring and unloving. If this were not negative enough, power actually adds to fear. Even a little power leads people to hoard their power and to obtain even more. Thankfully, we will soon recognize the negative aspects of power and how it adds to our fear. Institutional power – government and business – will be reduced, which will allow love to thrive. And personal ego-trip power will also diminish as the world transforms.

* * * * *

The reason we are on Earth is to become more spiritually aware. We do this with experiences we create from our beliefs. These beliefs come from our souls and are entwined with our life plans. Once we become aware of this, fear begins to diminish, and life becomes more meaningful. Each moment becomes an opportunity to experience and grow. Our old confusions, such as how to obtain social status and material wealth, become less important. The true reality of life begins to supersede the illusion of this lifetime.

Society is currently polluted with negativity, but this will soon change. Self-interest will change to common interest as we recognize the need to get along with each other. Spiritual awareness will lead people to begin sharing and living together. People will recognize that selfless interest is how we must live if we want harmony. We will no longer feel in competition with others, or the desire to have more than the next person.

I cannot talk about fear without talking about ego, which is our false identity. The ego is the part of our consciousness that confuses us into believing that we are real, and that the physical world is real. Our ego does everything in its power to prevent us from recognizing our divinity. It knows that once we become aware of the reality of God, we will no longer be under its spell.

Most of the world's population is under the spell of the ego, and thus lives in fear. Likewise, just about everyone is unaware of their divinity. Most people believe their current life is their first and only life. The ego has such control that the average person will not even consider metaphysical concepts. Most people would rather keep their current fears than introduce new fears into their lives.

I always find it fascinating that people can't read my books. Their ego won't let them! Their ego tells them that they don't believe this baloney and they stop reading, or they never start because of the subject matter.

People spend their lives supporting and maintaining the false identity that their ego created. Hence, the ego strives to maintain its false identity. For instance, it scares us into holding onto our current beliefs, because the ego does not like change, which can lead to a loss of control. Moreover, until ego is recognized for what it is in society, it will remain in control over us.

Our egos uses fear to control us. However, the moment we realize there is nothing to fear, the ego begins to lose control. Slowly, as we connect with our souls, our egos lose their power over us. Our higher self steps in and assumes control as we begin to live from spirit, using intuition. We switch control from the ego to the soul, and from an outer focus to an inner focus.

This switch from the ego to the soul is also a switch from living by fear to living by love. The entire world is about to make this switch. This is what the transformation of humanity is all about.

Love will manifest because that is our destiny. This manifestation began in the 1960s and will culminate with the beginning of a new civilization during our lifetime. Many people today are manifesting love instead of fear. As more people become aware, the numbers will increase.

* * * * *

Ambition is generally a sign of fear. Did you know that old souls are rarely materialistic or ambitious? They know intuitively, from many past lives, that inflating the ego is counter-productive to their soul, and that too much self-interest in satisfying the ego produces karma.

I am not suggesting that ambition is wrong. After all, I needed quite a bit to write this book. Ambition drives people to achieve their dreams and goals. Many souls incarnate with an abundance of ambition, which leads to very rewarding and fulfilling lives. And it is possible to achieve without infringing on the wills of others. Conversely, I am talking about when ambition causes too much self-interest. There is a difference between doing what comes naturally and seeking to satisfy the ego's yearnings.

We live in a time when satisfying the ego is pervasive – a hedonistic culture. This shall be replaced with satisfying the soul. Let me give an example. Two people decide to become doctors. The first loves her science classes and has wanted to be a doctor all her life. She truly desires to help people. The fact that doctors are respected and well paid is a secondary criterion.

The second person wants to be a doctor because it is prestigious, and he expects to get paid a lot of money and have a nice house. He has a huge ego and perceives himself as smarter and better than the average person. He sees being a doctor as the optimal job to satisfy his desire for a successful life.

What is the result? The first doctor perceives her patients as people in need. The second doctor perceives his patients as a means to an end. He is arrogant and full of self-interest. If he is criticized by another doctor, he becomes upset and lashes out, defensive at any attack on his identity. The first doctor views criticism as constructive and will do what she can to prevent a problem from happening again.

This example can be applied to any profession. When people's motives are strongly ego-based, they continuously force their wills upon others. They do not perceive others as their equal, but as people whose status is not on their level. And anyone who threatens their self-interest is perceived as a threat.

As you can see, self-interest does not usually spread love. In fact, too much self-interest prevents love. This comes from the ego. Too much self-interest causes a desire for control. From that comes the desire for power.

In the near future, enough people will be spiritually aware that society will begin to focus on humanity. The belief in separation will no longer be as strong as it is today. By the next generation, the majority of the world's population will perceive separation as an illusion.

People with too much self-interest will no longer be allowed to force their wills upon others. Whereas today young souls are in charge, in the near future, old souls will have a larger influence. The old souls will implement a love-based, humanitarian society.

* * * * *

Now let's talk about worry. Worry is basically the same thing as fear, yet to a lesser degree. Fear is the trepidation of an outcome that we do not desire. Is that not a good definition of worry?

Because we create our own reality by our thoughts, we actually promulgate negative outcomes by our worries. We can literally create what we worry about. Thus, there is a close connection between worry and negative experiences. This is why earlier, I wrote about remaining in a positive frame of mind and to expect good things.

To worry is to deny our connection to God. In the book *Emissary of Love*, by James Twyman, one of the psychic children states that our civilization does not believe God loves us and that all of our problems stem from that belief. In many respects, worry is the denial of God, which prevents a joyful life. In other words, it is the spiritual awareness of God that manifests harmony and therefore negates worry. Likewise, the lack of spiritual awareness manifests a lack of trust, which results in disharmony and an abundance of worry.

You might be thinking, how can a simple act of worry create negative experiences? Worry and fear are the nemeses of harmony. They are our favorite means of disrupting our harmony. Conversely, if we believe we are connected to God and that our lives are carefully pre-planned, we can trust that there is nothing to worry about.

My current morning hand prayer includes the following (it is number two out of ten): Have faith, trust the plan, truth the perfection.

This prayer reminds me each morning that my life is perfectly planned by a higher power. This is what helps me to reduce any worrying.

Worry denies that everything is okay, when in fact, everything is perfect. Worry is a projection that the next moment will not be what we desire, when in fact, everything we create is the manifestation of what we need. In other words, everyone is getting exactly what they need.

Worry and spiritual awareness do not go together. When we are spiritually aware, we realize that all experiences are created for a purpose and that the purpose is to learn from those experiences. To worry is to deny that we create the events in our lives. Worry is the belief that life is a series of random events.

To repeat, negative experiences, which lead to disharmony, are created from worry and fear. For instance, suppose you put yourself under enormous pressure to make sure a project at work goes smoothly. You neglect your wife and children while focusing on the project. When you are with friends, your mind is somewhere else and thinking about the project. When your wife asks for a short weekend trip, you say that it is not a good time. When your children ask that you come and watch them play soccer, you do not show up.

This example can be applied to many situations. When we worry with a chattering mind about any situation, the people around us are affected. Likewise, when we are clear-minded and peaceful, we spread love. When people we care about make a request, we respond with love.

Do you know why certain children love their parents intensely? It is because their parents have *always* been there to love them. Those children know their parents will satisfy their needs. They know their parents will *always* be ready to respond to their requests. Living a lifestyle of worrying is not conducive to satisfying those requests.

All relationships can be as loving as a parent-child relationship. To paraphrase my favorite college professor: a relationship is a relationship is a relationship. Any relationship can be based on love. Yes, a parent-child relationship creates a special bond, but any two people can give love back and forth. It is simply a matter of *always* responding to each other's needs. If we are busy worrying about our own needs, we have little to offer anyone else. When we are in a state of worry or fear, we are not able to respond.

Worry is actually a selfish emotion, and it comes directly from the ego. Worry is the result of not trusting God and denying our divinity. It is a reflection of our spiritual awareness, or lack thereof.

A simple way to reduce fear or worry is to remain present. When you are in the present moment with a quiet mind, the ego is held at bay, and your fear and worry are stymied. Try it! If your mind won't turn off, then begin to meditate on a daily basis to learn how to turn off your active mind – your ego. I have also found that exercise is a good way to quiet your mind.

Another way to reduce fear or worry is to embrace uncertainty. Accept everything that happens in your life as either a blessing or an opportunity. Moreover, remain positive at all times and in the present moment. Make the present moment your friend and not your enemy.

Here is another thing that you probably don't know. Fear uses up your energy. By reducing your fear, you are also freeing up an abundance of energy. Fear and worry require a great deal of energy. They are both energy drains. Let them go and free up this wasted energy. For example, have you ever noticed that you have more energy when you are on vacation? That is the one time when you tend to drop your worries.

CHAPTER TWELVE

Love and Hate

Love is the feeling that makes us feel alive. Love is not only an emotion, but the core of our being. It is the affectionate feeling we have for others as well as the root of our existence. It is our connection with our true self and our connection with others. In many respects, God *is* love.

One of the keys to finding spiritual awareness is love, affectionate love. The reason is that in order to come closer to God, we must love both ourselves and humanity. Learning to love ourselves usually starts with the awareness that we are eternal. Then, it is an easy leap to the realization that our lives are perfect. Next, we realize we are on a spiritual journey that will lead us to enlightenment. After that, we realize we have spirit guides helping us. After these realizations, loving ourselves is a natural outcome.

Once we have learned to love ourselves, we are ready to love other aspects of God: all of humanity as well as animals and nature. We also learn that love is the method of communication. Now when we communicate, we do it with an understanding that everyone is our equal. We realize that we create all of our encounters and that each has meaning. We begin to love whomever we are communicating with because we wish to share our understanding.

When we communicate from this viewpoint, we uplift the people with whom we interact. We actually spread love by doing this. By treating everyone as God, we spread love and harmony. Earlier, I called this the frequency of love.

To feel love in any situation, remain connected to your soul – living with one foot in this world and one foot connected to spirit. As Jesus said, "Of myself, I can do nothing." The moment we perceive the physical world as real is the moment we block love. When we are connected to spirit, we have the ability to feel love in any situation.

Have you noticed how love flows when you are around someone you love? How would you feel in Jesus' or Buddha's presence? Most likely, you would have an intense feeling of love. You can feel that kind of love in any situation. All you need to do is change your perceptions.

Love comes from the soul – the heart. By remembering who you are, it is easier to feel that love. Indeed, the more aware we are of God, the more that love manifests. Find God, and you will find love within you for everyone.

The rest of the chapter, I am going to discuss hate. Without love, hate is what we experience. It's not fun to read about, so I will keep it short.

In the absence of love is hate, or at the very least, an aversion (dislike) to something or someone. As our spiritual awareness expands, our love expands, and hatred steadily disappears. For instance, there was not an ounce of hatred in Jesus. He loved everyone and everything.

Note: Aversion (dislike) is not necessarily hate, but it is the absence of love. This section focuses more on hate. However, any resolution used to remove hate will also resolve any aversion issues.

* * * * *

Hate and love are closely related. Hatred arises from anger, which arises from resentment, which arises from expectation. When someone or something does not meet our expectations, we may become resentful and then angry, which is hate.

Hatred is a judgment that we do not like someone or something. Just as love has varying levels of intensity, so does hatred. For instance, if someone pulls out in front of you when you are driving and you have to avoid a collision, how angry do you become? Do you call the person names or honk your horn in displeasure?

This example applies to just about any situation where we become upset. Getting upset is due to an expectation of some kind. In the previous example, the expectation could have been to share the road with only safe drivers. The stronger the expectation, the more upset we might become when encountering unsafe drivers.

Events in our lives happen for a reason. When an expectation is shattered, it is actually an opportunity to learn, and not an opportunity to become livid and resent someone. For instance, when something happens that you do not expect, that is an ideal time to reflect on the meaning and purpose behind the incident. It is an opportunity to discover the beliefs you are using to create your life. I often ask myself, "Why did I create that?"

Because we are not yet spiritual masters, most of us have resentment in our lives and react to situations in a negative manner. Resentment is a subtle form of hatred (and reveals our belief in separation). When resentment is present, hatred is not far behind.

These reactions are by degree. Some reactions are intense, and others are mild forms of resentment. They all reveal a lack of love (and a belief in separation). An enlightened person who exudes love rarely reacts with resentment. He or she knows that unconditional love means to allow other people to make their own decisions, and that life is unfolding as it is supposed to.

People want love in their lives. When they do not receive it, they resent something or someone in response. The perceived lack of love provides an impetus for hate. When we see someone upset and displaying hatred, it's because, either consciously or subconsciously, the person perceives a lack of love. It is not easy comforting that person. The best thing we can do is set an example. When we recognize that our lives are perfect, there is no reason to lose our equilibrium.

Hatred is a form of spiritual ignorance. Hatred is pervasive today because there is little spiritual awareness on the planet at this time. It is so rampant that most people cannot get through a typical day without encountering hatred or feeling it.

Hatred is dominant today because a love of humanity by individuals is lacking (or a feeling of oneness). The result is that people are constantly upset and revealing hatred, anger, or resentment. Just listen to talk radio or read social media! As stated before, the higher the expectation, the more intense the reaction.

In the chapter on harmlessness, I stated that to be harmless, we have to face situations with equanimity. In other words, rather than react with hatred, we can react with love and compassion. This is not the norm today. People are constantly reacting angrily. Anger feeds anger, leading to more anger. The result is a world gripped by anger, which is hatred.

The root cause of hatred is the belief in separation – the lack of awareness that we are all consciously connected. Have you wondered why people hate criminals so intensely and feel no affinity with them? For instance, how upset would you be if you returned home and found you had been burglarized? The typical response is anger: "How dare someone take my stuff?"

A spiritual person would perceive the situation with a degree of equanimity. A rare, enlightened person would not react at all. Being burglarized or victimized happens for a reason. The apparent randomness of such events is actually orderly. There is no randomness in life. We create it all. Moreover, nothing is taken from us unless we want it to be taken – at the soul level of consciousness. Not our possessions, and especially not our lives.

Criminals are generally hated for their past discretions and are never truly forgiven. Those who commit felonies, especially violent crimes, are pariahs in society. This reflects our strong social belief in separation and the prevalence of judging others.

Today in America, most felons do not get a second chance. One felony, and it becomes difficult to find a good job, which generally requires a background check.

Hatred arises from beliefs, and our beliefs determine our experiences. For example, people become angry when they believe in bad guys. Instead of realizing we are all on a spiritual journey of eternal life, many people believe that certain other people are destined for hell and, thus, deserve condemnation.

Another aspect of hatred is the expectation of a fulfilled life. For most people, anything that stands in the way of fulfillment is resented. From this perspective, society believes it is okay to become upset if life goes awry. Anger is perceived as normal. This is why people are always fighting for their rights and suing each other. Every day we read in the newspaper about another lawsuit concerning rights of some kind. When expectations are broken, many people call a lawyer.

The concept of fairness is strongly held in society, even though most things in life are not fair. Everyone demands to be treated fairly, even if we cannot agree on what is fair. As a result, if someone perceives he or she is not treated fairly, the normal response is that the person claims the right to be upset.

Because the concept of fairness is difficult to define, people define it any way they choose. As previously stated, people claim their right to define fairness on their own terms. "You cannot treat me like that! I deserve respect!" With all of the hypocrisy and irony surrounding fairness, you have to admire God's sense of humor.

When an expectation of fairness is violated, people become upset. This can be anything from a simple statement, an accusation, or an act of some kind. From a spiritual standpoint, the concept of fairness has no validity. Everyone's life is perfect, and everyone is creating their own reality. This is a drastically different viewpoint than the way society currently views fairness.

There is a large chasm between the metaphysical spiritual perspectives of fairness and the currently accepted beliefs. Likewise, there is a chasm between the spiritual perspective that we are all one and the widely accepted belief that we are all separate. The result of these divergent beliefs is a lack of love and the manifestation of hatred.

The chasm in beliefs is extremely wide between current society and metaphysical ideas. Today, if someone thinks you hold divergent beliefs from theirs, you can be killed simply from hatred. Society has become that dangerous. It also reveals how badly society needs to change, and to wake up to the truth that can create peace on Earth.

* * * * *

Because most people have little spiritual knowledge, they walk around in a state of anxiety, afraid that fulfillment in their life is going to be stifled. They believe that their lives are random, and that other people are impinging on their happiness. They feel that their only recourse is to attempt to defend themselves against the onslaught of humanity, often by giving in to anger.

Any perceived infringement often creates a reaction. Anything from slight indignation, to a confrontation, to full-scale anxiety, to a trip to a lawyer's office, or, perhaps violence, can result. We react according to our beliefs and are often at each other's throats. That needs to change, and the only way it can happen is by changing our beliefs.

When I lived in Los Angeles, I wondered why people were so distant from each other. Strangers rarely talked, and neighbors were quiet and interacted very little. In the five years I lived there, I met a total of three neighborhood families. I discovered that people prefer to keep to themselves. People live in isolation because they do not love each other. It is as simple as that. In the absence of love, there is hate, or at the very least, aversion (some form of dislike).

Because the vast majority of people live by self-will, hatred (or aversion) is rampant. Living by self-will is denying God, which leads to resentment because we have so many expectations. I stated in a previous chapter that people are harming each other constantly. Hatred is one of the ways we do harm.

Hatred does not have to exist. As society becomes spiritually aware, I believe hatred will become a thing of the past. There will be no place for hatred in a society based on oneness.

CHAPTER THIRTEEN

Decision Making

Krishnamurti said that only the mind that is confused chooses, but a mind that sees clearly has only one choice. Thus, he believed that we never have to make decisions by selecting from various options. Through what he called *passive awareness*, we can let life unfold in an intuitive manner, with the correct choice always revealing itself. Instead of directing our lives through left-brain, logical decision-making, we allow spirit to direct us intuitively.

When I first read Krishnamurti, I did not understand him. However, years later, I get it. The soul knows the path to take. The key is learning how to listen to your higher self and spirit guides, which takes some practice.

The key to decision-making is living by intuition, connected to our higher self (the soul) and our spirit guides. This allows us to live a spiritual life in which we constantly communicate with the other side of the veil. This leads to decision-making in accordance with God's will, which is the will of our higher self.

Another key to decision-making is knowing who we are and where we are going – our life's plan. In other words, we need to understand exactly what is occurring in our lives at this moment. Krishnamurti said that in order to understand ourselves, we must first understand *what* is in our lives. Once we understand our relationships in life – romance, work, friends – we know who we are and where we are. Without this knowledge, we are confused and incapable of making good decisions.

We need to see the big picture and come to recognize how our present lives have meaning and purpose and are teaching us the lessons we need. We need to see everything in our lives and then connect the dots. Then we can accept our lessons as a part of our spiritual journey, and it is easier to make decisions. Moreover, we can then forgive ourselves and let go of the past. We no longer need to try to attain something. We can accept things as they are.

After recognizing that there is a purpose to our lives, we become more aware of what we are doing. We begin focusing more on today, and our lives become more important to us. We begin to realize that whatever we are doing makes perfect sense and that there are reasons for our current situation.

Once you accept that your life is perfect, you are able to focus on today and let tomorrow take care of itself. The ego must be humbled to accept this point of view. Make a mental note to yourself that you have everything you need and to accept the lessons that you are learning. Acknowledge your lessons as opportunities rather than as trials, and that you chose this for a reason.

Use your intuition at all times, and only make decisions when they *feel* right. Quiet your mind, and do not try to find the answers with your mind. Instead, try to *feel* your answers. The correct answers are often subtle nudges from your soul, and not blatant choices. Let them come at their own pace. Delay decisions until you feel comfortable with your insights.

Intuition comes from the soul. When we make decisions based on intuition, this takes us closer to our true self. For instance, instead of complaining when you are upset, remain calm and realize that the correct attitude is equanimity. Instead of complaining, allow your life to unfold.

Jesus was an example of making decisions from the soul level. He understood God's will and made decisions that coincided with that will. He lived moment to moment, responding to subtle feelings that he felt from his soul. His heart was open and full of love. He did not think in terms of the social norms of his day. He focused on how he felt inside, regardless of the opinions of others.

An avatar, or enlightened person, knows that the greater good is more important than the individual self. In fact, to an avatar, the concept of an individual self has lost its meaning. Instead, an awareness of the greater good has become apparent and more relevant.

When we realize the significance of a oneness that exists, our decisions and choices reflect that awareness. For instance, we can decide to make only positive decisions that create positive effects on humanity. With such an affirmation, the concept of self loses its meaning. Instead, we become an aspect of God. We literally surrender to the will of God – love and harmony. This is where the concept of service comes in. Instead of living selfishly, we live for others, *all* others, which is humanity. This is how we give service to God. Our own needs lose significance.

This brings us to an important point: accepting your life as perfect is realizing that your life has no purpose other than to satisfy God's will. With this awareness, you literally live to satisfy God's will.

Here is another truth bomb I will drop. The meaning of life is to become a conscious instrument of the divine consciousness. This means that we need to surrender our will to that of the divine consciousness.

Each of us has the choice to live by our own will and rebel against God, or to live for ALL and follow God's will. When we focus on the past or future, we are focusing on our wills (the ego). When we focus on now (the present moment), we are focusing on God's will. In the present moment, the mind is quiet, and we can feel the soul.

There is no need, other than ego gratification, to think about the past or future, because God's will occurs in the present moment. Only the present moment provides a link with God. This is perhaps the most important thing you can learn from this book.

Once we realize that we have guidance to live by God's will, we should live with gratitude that this is possible. We shouldn't mock God and ignore this possibility and follow our ego. Instead, we should marginalize our ego by living in the present moment. Moreover, we should see life as a blessing and become an example who spreads the light. We should try to become the best version of ourselves, which is a conscious instrument of the divine consciousness. Note that the ONLY thing that prevents this are naivete and the ego.

When we focus on our will, we are living from ego. By doing this, we are just lost in the illusion of life. From this perspective, it is pointless to focus on our own will, other than to learn that it is pointless.

Our lives have meaning only in the context of God's will. However, we can never fully understand the meaning of our lives because we can never fully know God's will. This is why it makes sense to live by God's will rather than our own, and why it makes sense to forget about tomorrow, and instead allow God to show us the way.

We can rebel against the will of God, or attempt to follow it. God is continuously attempting to create a loving and harmonious planet, yet our decisions affect the outcome and progress. We are either helping that progress with our positive actions or hindering it with negative actions. I like to use the analogy that we are either fixing the problem (following God's will), or we part of the problem (following our will).

This brings us to an example of how to follow God's will. Say you are a college student. Decision-making is quite simple in that situation. All you need to do is focus on *being* a student. All of your decisions should revolve around being a student. Thus, follow your intuition within this context. The more you focus on being a student, the more your intuition will lead you. Do not think about the past or future, because those thoughts will only complicate the situation.

Each day should be easy and should flow. The moment you wake up each morning, you should know what is on your day's agenda. For instance, you might have a class in the morning, homework in the afternoon, then a job at night. Each day's plan should be in your mind when you wake up. Nothing should get in the way unless it feels intuitively right to modify your daily plan.

The days should flow together, one into the next, with a common connection between them. If the days are not flowing together, then you are not focusing on being a student. For instance, if you are not going to class or doing your homework, you are not focusing, and you are not *being* a student.

Life is about *focusing*. The better we focus, the easier life is. A question arises: What are you focusing on? *What* is in your life? It is not that difficult to understand what you are currently doing. All you have to do is look at everything you are currently doing on a daily basis. Do not analyze *why* you are doing something. Accept what you find without judgment. The goal is to see the big picture and understand your life.

Analyze *what* you are doing and attempt to understand what you are focusing on. Do not try to change anything. Keep doing the same things until you understand what you are focusing on. Most likely, you will find that you are not focused on anything. You will probably find that your focus is scattered and that you do not know what to focus on, other than possibly parenthood, a relationship, or work.

Once you learn how to focus, it will not matter what you select to be or do with your life. No matter what you select, your awareness will increase. You will find yourself in touch with your soul. Why? Because once you tell your soul what to focus on, you can work as a team with your spirit.

The only way to connect to your soul is to quit being scattered – with a chattering mind – and begin to focus on something. You have to find a way to live in the present moment connected to your soul. And the only way to do that is to focus on something. The example above of the student was a perfect example. By *being* a student, you are able to lock into your soul and be guided toward graduation. All you need is intent and focus.

Focus your energy, and today will take care of itself. And if you have harmony and joy today, you will likely have harmony and joy tomorrow as well. If you have a connection to your higher self today, then you will also have it tomorrow as well.

If you do not understand what you are currently focusing on, then your ego is in control. It is easy to figure out how your ego is controlling you. Slow down. Start looking at how you live on a daily basis. What are your desires? Do you have a strong hedonistic urge to satisfy cravings? Did you know that desire is the destroyer and that all suffering comes from craving? Don't let temptations ruin your life. Desire is the telltale sign that the ego is in charge.

Learn this lesson right now: desire is the destroyer, and disinterest is the redeemer. How can you live by God's will if your desires run your life? Note that it isn't your desires that are running your life. It is your ego that is pushing your desire buttons. See your ego for what it really is: an obstacle to spiritual awareness.

Do a life assessment. Notice the people you have relationships with and the problems (if any) that exist in each relationship. Notice the problems in your life. Notice *what* you are doing on a daily basis. Notice what you aren't doing but want to do.

This assessment will create an understanding of who you are. Carefully review if this is how you want to live your life, or if there are some changes you would like to make. Ask yourself if you want to serve God and humanity or continue to be controlled by your ego. If you are ready to attempt to serve humanity, then find something to focus on that will serve that purpose. Note that this does not have to be something that saves the world. One option is simply to set a better example and prepare for the moment when God opens a door for your service to humanity.

God is always looking for volunteers to play a role that leads to more love and harmony on the planet. The biblical phrase, "Many are called, but few are chosen," fits here. God is looking for volunteers. We are constantly auditioning for roles given to us by the Director. This is why our life can take dramatic turns. God will tap on our shoulder and give us a new role.

You might think you have free will to change your role, but God's will and the grand plan will dictate the outcome. God has a hand in every role we choose and how we play our roles. Moreover, it is our beliefs and intent that lead to the roles we play.

For full disclosure, many people miss opportunities because their ego will get in the way. You may have the potential to play a specific role this lifetime, but that does not necessarily mean you will get the part. Ambivalence causes us to stray from being focused. For instance, college students often spend as much time doing social activities as they do studying. Ambivalence is why we have trouble listening to our intuition. We hear and feel the cues, but we do not act. The mind becomes scattered and unfocused, allowing the ego too much control. Instead of trusting God, we trust our egos (our false identities).

Ambivalence is actually a lack of awareness. Conversely, if you focus on your daily affairs, you can be aware of God's will in your life. You can be passionate and intense about your life. You can feel *alive*.

When you have focus, little things take on importance. A wink from an old man, the smile of a child, the friendliness of a stranger, can all bring a smile to your face. Such events can bring you joy and a passion for life.

When we recognize that each day is an opportunity, our ambivalence begins to fade. We begin to acknowledge the importance of the little things. This occurs by recognizing God's will in our lives, and a desire to spread love and harmony in the world. Decision-making then is easy. We go from one event to the next listening to our hearts.

Ambivalence comes from the belief that the little things in life do not matter, and that life is a series of random events. But when you are aware that the little things do matter, everything becomes important, from noticing a kindness, to saying good morning. In fact, life is about the little things.

Everything that happens throughout the day is important. In essence, there are no little things. Everything is important.

* * * * *

We often make decisions with the intent of creating our personal happiness. However, with the right perception, happiness has nothing to do with your decisions. Happiness is a choice. If you perceive life as an incredible gift from God – to have this opportunity to expand your awareness – then you should be so grateful that it provides happiness. Moreover, happiness is not the result of getting what you want, but of receiving what you need. The difference is in perception, in recognizing that your life is perfect.

We are here to learn spiritual lessons. Your higher self and spirit guides are shaping your life to help you learn those lessons. When you understand this, you make decisions based on how you *feel* – living intuitively – and what you believe you are here to do. Decision-making takes on a whole new perspective once you become aware of the reality of life.

CHAPTER FOURTEEN

Self-Responsibility

Once we become aware of *who* we are (God), our lifestyles change. Life takes on a new meaning. Frivolous behavior loses its appeal, and we no longer act irresponsibly. We become serious-minded and self-responsible as we begin to respect our divinity. We become interested in understanding *why* we are here and *what* we came to do. We are no longer able to ignore the ramifications of our actions. We have come to realize that our actions have reactions, and that every act and every thought leads to an outcome.

Right now, as you are reading this material, you are creating ramifications. In many respects, this book is an initiation. This action will cause reactions, such as inspiring you to read additional spiritual material, or talking to others about what you have read.

Once we get on a spiritual path, we become self-responsible and self-reliant. This happens as we begin to identify with God's will. We learn to listen to our heart for guidance. We become aware that we are creating our reality by our beliefs and that our life has always been predicated by our beliefs.

Once we become self-reliant, it is amazing how serious we become. We no longer react to other people's expectations. We recognize that they do not know what is good for us, and that only we do. We no longer react when someone verbally attacks us. We recognize that people are interested only in our reactions, or to stimulate their own egos.

Once we become aware of *who* we are, we realize that we must make our own decisions that affect our spiritual path. Our lives switch from an outer focus to an inner focus. The physical world becomes secondary to our inner connection. This inner connection guides us to our own unique life experiences. These experiences expand our awareness and help us grow spiritually.

As we grow, we stop relying on others. We become self-reliant and inner-directed. Our growth depends on connecting with our guides and higher self. This inner connection separates us from the physical world. This connection is strictly our own, and we must find it on our own.

We are essentially alone in the world except for our higher self and guides who provide our connection to the higher plane. Family and friends can try to help with advice, but no one can make our decisions for us. *We* have to do it. Because of this isolation, our only link with the higher plane is to be inner guided.

Once we are inner guided, the world becomes no longer real to us, or less significant. We begin to perceive life from our inner connection. This feels strange at first because we perceive everything as an illusion, even our relationships. In essence, we perceive life as a dream, although a dream with ramifications.

This is where self-reliance and self-responsibility come in. Once we realize we are alone to direct our own lives from this inner connection and that everything else is a prop – like in a stage play – for our growth. We come to realize how important life really is, and the seriousness of life becomes apparent.

The more aware we become of the inner spiritual realities, the more serious and self-responsible we become. This seriousness is not directed towards achievement or the pursuit of ego gratification. Instead, we live with the understanding that we are trying to align with God's will and fulfill our life's purpose.

Once you grasp your role – your life's purpose – you become confident that you can play it. This subtle confidence diminishes your fear. In the process, you become serious and self-reliant to those with whom you interact. Being nonchalant and frivolous has lost its allure. You do everything from the perspective that God – your higher self – is watching and pointing the way.

* * * * *

Self-responsibility and karma go hand in hand. To review, karma is the result of our actions. Whether we harm someone or are nice, our actions have a consequence. This is karma. Every one of us is constantly creating karma with our actions. Our experiences today are the result of karma from past actions, whether in this life or previous lives. Everything is recorded (in the Akashic records), and everything has an impact.

We are each responsible for ourselves. We create our own karma and must resolve our negative karma on our own. This is why self-responsibility is important. It can be the difference between resolving our past karma and creating more negative karma.

When this life ends, you will have accumulated karma. It is inevitable. The karma that accumulates will be both positive and negative. You will then plan your next life based on that accumulation.

The very concept of karma implies that self-responsibility is a valuable trait. Resolving our negative karma is the path to spiritual awareness, and once we begin a spiritual path, living with self-responsibility becomes the norm.

Have you connected the dots and recognized why negative behavior (often called evil) steadily recedes? As the soul evolves, it recognizes that negative karma is only self-sabotage. Conversely, it recognizes that soul growth with an emphasis on love is the correct path.

Our inner connection to God is what keeps us from creating more negative karma. Moreover, our self-responsibility is how we respect God's will. In many respects, we become self-responsible to honor God. This is analogous to Priests and Nuns living without sin to honor God. Living a pure life, free of temptation, is the ultimate outcome for one who is enlightened. Although purity is not generally obtainable, living more responsibly with integrity is the result of anyone on a spiritual path.

* * * * *

What does it mean to be self-responsible? We listen to our hearts, and no matter where our hearts lead, we follow. We must be true to ourselves, which is the same thing as trusting our hearts. As a self-responsible person, we create our own value systems and a strong sense of direction for our lives. We get to know who we are and what we believe. We learn what fits in our lives and what does not. We become more methodical and careful in our thoughts. We begin to understand why we do what we do and the importance of pursuing our interests. Increasingly, how we feel about our lives becomes more important, and what others think loses relevance.

Our perceptions and beliefs change when we become inner-directed. One of these changes is that our worldly relationships become *secondary*. This idea is contrary to the conventional wisdom of being responsible to others first, especially in intimate relationships. However, by being responsible to ourselves *first*, we are also responsible to others. By honoring ourselves first, we not only create a strong connection with God, but a responsibility to others as well. Before we can have a relationship with another, we must first have a relationship with God. That relationship must come first.

Once we obtain this inner awareness, self-responsibility becomes the norm in our lifestyles. We allow no one to tell us how to live, because we know intuitively what we need. We become aware of God's plan, or at least a general outline. We begin to grasp the flow of life, where things are heading, and how we fit in. This makes it easier to be self-responsible for our roles. We can either follow the instructions of our higher self by being self-responsible, or we can follow our egos. By being self-responsible, we have the opportunity to work more closely with our higher self. This can lead to our lives improving as we receive a more favorable role.

I have found that the more self-responsible I am, the more my life flows. As the saying goes, nothing is better proof than experience. Likewise, when I do not follow my heart, my life gets out of balance, and I have to deal with the consequences.

It may seem that by focusing on being self-responsible we are being selfish. I do not believe this is true. Sacrificing our personal will to follow God's will is the opposite of selfishness. Selfishness is when we follow our own will (ego).

One channeled source that I have read compares life to sacrificial service. This is an interesting way of saying that the key to life is following God's will. In many respects, being self-responsible does feel like a sacrifice. Waking up in the morning and knowing God is in charge of your life can feel like servitude. That is true until you realize that *you* chose this life.

In many ways, I feel like my life is not in my own hands and that I am following orders. For instance, I often contemplate possible experiences. I will think about going on vacations, buying something, doing something, or calling someone. Inevitably, I only go ahead with these ideas only when my heart agrees, and if it *feels* right. If my heart says no, then it's a no-go.

I'll give you one example. I have never owned a sports car, even though I've always wanted one. My spirit guides have told me that this particular incarnation (lifetime) is not about having fun and to focus on what is important. Basically, they have said no!

Personally, I do not feel as if I am sacrificing. I feel empowered. Following my heart gives me incredible inner strength and peace. Likewise, if I ignore my heart and stubbornly follow my ego, I become incredibly vulnerable. My life can easily head down a path I would rather not experience. My intuition generally saves me from such hardships. I hear a voice that says, "No!" And I am responsible enough to follow heed.

It may seem to some of you that I live in fear by following God's plan for my life, and always following orders. However, I do not feel that way. My experience has proven to me that God's will (my higher self) influences my life. So why fight it? Also, by following God's will, my life contains harmony, contentment, and an abundance of love.

By being self-responsible, we are actually taking advantage of the opportunity to live God's will. The whole point of life is remembering who we are (God). Being self-responsible helps to reveal our true self and God's will. Let me give you another example. If you have a job to do, you have choices on how to perform that job. The more responsible you feel about performing your tasks, the more judicious the outcome. Thus, by being responsible, you are more diligent. This analogy applies to living God's will. The more responsible we feel to live God's will, the more diligent we are in our lives.

The person who does only enough to get by in life does not feel responsible to God or to themself. Not because he or she is rejecting God, but because they are oblivious to God's will. Thus, the paradox: how can people be self-responsible if they aren't even aware they *are* God? Or that God's will exists and is accessible?

People who are not self-responsible have forgotten who they are. The result is a denial of God's will and a profusion of irresponsibility in their lives. Moreover, as I have stated many times in this book, they believe in separation, which is a false belief.

Here is a true story about being irresponsible due to a lack of awareness of God's will. The son of an extremely wealthy family was told that if he married his girlfriend, he would no longer be welcome in the family. He was threatened not only with losing his inheritance, but future family contact. Until the engagement there were no problems, since he was allowed to have girlfriends. The son was handsome, well-liked, well-educated, and a professional. Likewise, his girlfriend matched his traits, although she was not rich. There was nothing to imply a reason for his family's intransigence other than her lack of wealth.

Despite his family's objections, he chose to marry his girlfriend. A few of his relatives showed up at the wedding, but his immediate family refused to come, even though the ceremony was held near the family home. This happened in Southern California and was reported by the *Los Angeles Times*.

What does this event tell us? First, it is an extreme, and extremes always teach something about society. The same factors in this incident are at work throughout society. When an entire family turns their back on a son and brother, that is an act of spiritual irresponsibility. This is the epitome of self-responsibility gone awry. All of them blocked their intuition and followed their ego.

This story is an example of a family's lack of spirituality. Their actions created karma for each of them. In their futures, they will have to amend. For instance, someone they love may neglect them harshly. Eventually, they will get to feel the same heartache. Probably not in this lifetime, but very likely in another.

All actions create karma, to an extent. This example is extreme and makes it easy for us to see the ramifications of one's actions. In this way, this incident is a lesson for all of us.

Previously, I talked about harmlessness, and that when people live by their own will instead of God's will, inevitably they create harm. This newspaper story is an example of creating harm by living stubbornly by our own will instead of for the highest good.

This family had power because of their wealth and influence. From this power, they exercised their will to ostracize their son. I think they believed they had to do this in order to maintain their way of life. They invest in America, create jobs, and donate millions of dollars. They consider themselves the backbone of America.

Many members of such elite families believe it is acceptable to ostracize behavior they deem improper. However, in doing so, they are unaware that this is spiritually irresponsible and that they are creating negative karma for themselves and society.

The belief in separation is what causes people to act irresponsibly. To most people, separation is not only real but the very thing that determines how society is formed. Most people honestly believe that people rise to the top because of their separateness. This family did not accept their son's choice for a wife because she was not one of them. She was perceived as socially below them, and separate in the wrong way.

This brings up a topic that is irritating to me, which is the concept of staying in your lane. This is a conservative idea that some people are better than others and deserve their elite status (and big houses). Thus, they are above others because of their personality traits, intelligence, and societal position. Rich people tend to buy into this belief of feeling special and want those below them to honor their societal positions and stay in their lane. It is the idea that some people are better than others, and thereby deserve their spoils. Basically, they think they are better than you. That is the idea that gave rise to the Illuminati's rise to power. This is pure hubris and why the Bible says the poor will inherit the Earth.

The family mentioned in the example above is a group of young souls who are learning lessons about ego, such as how to deal with power and material possessions. Empires are generally run by young souls. Mature souls and old souls have already learned those lessons. Mature souls are learning lessons about emotions and relationships. Old souls are learning lessons about unconditional love and their relationships with God.

* * * * *

Very soon, events will transpire that bring about a transformation of humanity. It will not be long before most people become spiritually responsible. Turning one's back on another will be rare. People will pull together. Families will pull together. Friends will cherish friendships. Human relationships will become very important, and money will lose much of its significance.

Chaotic events will soon transpire and overwhelm many. This is another good reason to be self-responsible and self-reliant. How chaotic will things be? Over the next decade, society will have changed so dramatically that many people will be in a state of shock. What is coming is nothing short of incredible. (Refer to my book *The Path Forward*). The transformation will be so complete that there will be very little resemblance to how the world is currently organized.

Self-responsibility and self-reliance will help us adapt to this complete transformation of humanity. When we know how to use our inner connection to our higher self and spirit guides, we are unafraid because we know that we will be given guidance. We will open our hearts to divine guidance and trust that our lives will be guided safely and harmoniously.

CHAPTER FIFTEEN

Know Yourself

Before you can answer the important questions about your life, you need to know who you are. Fortunately, I can tell you how to do this, and it's not that difficult. It will take some effort on your part, along with some time and money, but all you need is the intent to find out.

I don't think you can know yourself in a short period of time. It will probably take at least a year and, perhaps, many years. The reason for the long timeframe is that part of getting to know yourself is finding your soul. I'm saving this for the last chapter because it can be considered part two of getting to know yourself.

In actuality, there are two parts to our self. There is the ego personality, and the soul. In this chapter, I am going to focus on learning how to know your ego personality. There are several methods that make this possible. I will describe each one below.

Astrology

Your natal chart is the best place to start. This is a report of approximately twenty-five pages that explains many of your personality traits. Hopefully, you know your place of birth and time of birth. If you do, then you are ready to have this report created. You will have dozens of choices to choose from on the Internet. They are all pretty much the same, although they will vary in quality.

Do some research and read the reviews before purchasing a natal chart. Consider using a professional astrologer for a one-on-one natal chart reading. This is more expensive than a printout, but worth it. Ideally, I would recommend getting a printout from a quality website and having a professional astrologer analyze your chart. That is what I did. Read the printout first, so that you are prepared for the astrologer with questions.

A professional astrologer is not necessary and perhaps a bit of overkill. However, you will learn a few things that are useful to know that you might not learn from the printout.

You are going to want to read this report thoroughly, and more than once. Then, after you have read it, you are going to want to do some additional research on your Sun sign, rising sign, and moon sign. The reason for the extra research is that these three placements have a big impact on your personality, as well as your compatibility with others.

For some of you, the natal chart report might be enough information. But if you are passionate about your spiritual journey, you will probably want to dig a bit deeper to find out more information. This deeper dive will lead you to understand your natal horoscope more thoroughly.

The starting point for a deeper dive is to read and learn the traits of *all* of the Sun signs. You may be asking yourself, why do I need to know the traits of all of the signs? What is the importance of that? Well, as you will come to know, your personality is comprised of many of the signs. Plus, the people in your life will comprise the rest.

When you know the traits of all of the signs, it allows you to understand the signs that impact you in a more substantial way. This may sound counterintuitive, but by knowing what you are *not* exposes you to what you *are*. Make sense? If not, it will after you learn the traits of all the signs.

Another reason that it is important to know our astrological traits is that you are uncovering the truth about yourself. This truth is already known by your soul. This allows both of you to speak in a language that you both understand. When I uncovered this, it blew my mind as to the possibilities. The soul kind of smiles and says, "It was nice of you to catch up."

Some of you may have just rolled your eyes after reading that last sentence. But your relationship with your soul is about to take on a whole new meaning after you read this book. You may think that the soul cannot communicate with you in a profound way; well, I'm here to tell you that it can. Moreover, the more you can speak its language, the more it will communicate with you.

If you go for a deeper dive, you will want to understand the elements of each sign, which are fire, water, earth, and air. Then, you will want to understand the qualities of each sign, which are fixed, cardinal, and mutable. After that, you will want to learn the planetary rulers of each sign. That is the bare minimum, in my opinion, if you want to understand the basics of astrology.

If you know the basics of astrology, that should be enough for you to communicate with the soul about your personality traits. It is difficult for me to put into words how the soul will use that common understanding about yourself to guide you. This common understanding becomes a pathway that the soul can use in profound ways. One of those pathways is to guide you to learn more about yourself. Once you find a way to connect with the soul, it's like opening up a door to additional pathways.

For those you who want to understand more about astrology, there is a lot to learn. It is a science, in my opinion, although today, it is still considered a pseudoscience and is not taught in accredited colleges. In the future, I expect astrologers to be licensed. You can take private astrology classes to become an expert if you feel compelled to learn more. You could even become an astrologer. I personally was content with the basics in order to learn my personality traits.

My sun sign is Pisces, my moon is Sagittarius, and my rising sign is Cancer. I have learned the qualities, elements, and planetary rulers of each. For instance, Pisces is a mutable, water sign, ruled by Neptune. I know the qualities, elements, and planetary rulers of all of the signs. This helps me to know not only my own personality traits, but those of others.

Once, I had a professional astrologer give me a natal horoscope reading. She said that my potential for understanding spirituality was unlimited. This is the reason why I started writing spiritual philosophy only a year after I began my spiritual journey. Everything that I was reading felt like a remembrance. I was remembering knowledge that I had learned from past lifetimes.

This is the reason why some people pick up music, painting, languages, and other skills with relative ease at an early age. Spiritual knowledge was right there in my natal horoscope. That was just the beginning of what there was to discover about myself. There are nine planets (if you count Pluto), plus the sun and moon. Each of these is placed somewhere in your natal chart, and each impacts your personality traits.

Let me give you a list of what you need to learn for the astrology basics:

1. The traits of each sign.
2. The quality (fixed, cardinal, mutable) of each sign.
3. The element (air, fire, water, earth) of each sign.
4. The planetary ruler of each sign.
5. The traits of each planet.

I have found that my sun sign, rising sign, and moon have the biggest impact on my personality. So, spend more time analyzing those. When you integrate the traits of those three, it will give you a good perspective about yourself.

Numerology

All of us have several numbers associated with our birthday and name. I like to use six numbers, which are the following:

1. **Lifepath**: Add together all of the digits of your date of birth into a single digit. Mine is 3 + 1 + 8 + 1 + 9 + 6 + 0 = 28. Then convert double digits to a single digit by adding those together. 2 + 8 = 10. 1 + 0 = 1.

2. **Birthday**: Add together your birth day into a single digit. For example, if you were born on the 29th, it would be 2 + 9 = 11. 1 + 1 = 2.

3. **Attitude**: Add together your birth day and birth month into a single digit.

4. **Personality**: Add together the consonants in your full name using the Pythagoras method of converting letters to numbers. Convert the total into a single digit.

5. **Soul**: Add together the vowels in your full name using the Pythagoras method of converting letters to numbers. Convert the total into a single digit.

6. **Power**: Combine your personality and soul numbers into a single digit.

Comparing these six numbers with someone else is remarkably accurate for determining compatibility with other people. However, you need to know how to compare. With a little bit of research, you can figure it out. Basically, if you have a lot of even numbers, then you will be more compatible with someone who also has a lot of even numbers.

Just like an astrological sign, each number has its own meaning. The number that probably has the biggest impact on your personality is your lifepath. My lifepath number is 28/1. After reading the characteristics of a 28/1, it made a lot of sense what drove my behavior.

You should learn the characteristics of each number, and you should add up the lifepath number for those people closest to you. Each data point that you collect gives you that much more information about yourself and someone else. In my opinion, someone's lifepath number is just as significant as their Sun sign.

If you have not read the traits of your lifepath number in Dan Millman's book, *The Life You Were Born to Live,* then you are missing out on understanding yourself. It's only a few pages for each lifepath, so you can read them at the library or Barnes &Noble in a few minutes.

Knowing your lifepath number, as well as your other numbers, gives you more data points into understanding your personality traits. I have mostly odd numbers, which makes me an introverted, creative type of person. Odd numbers also make my life more challenging and difficult. It is much easier to have an even-numbered lifepath. I also have five squares in my natal horoscope, and each square creates challenges or obstacles in your life. Knowing this gives me perspective on my challenges.

There are different ways to approach numerology. I have given you an overview, but if you read a book on numerology, you will learn more. I think the lifepath number is the most important, but you will find that other people have different opinions. I have not spent a lot of time on numerology. Only enough to learn my traits.

Science of the Cards

I didn't know about the Science of the Cards until 2006. In fact, most people have never heard of it. I was lucky to have met an expert who exposed me to it. When we met, one of the first things she said was what day is your birthday. After I told her March 18th, she replied, "You are a five of diamonds. One of my best friends is also a five of diamonds." I had no idea what she was talking about. I had been on my spiritual journey for several years and had done a prolific amount of reading, but had never come across the Science of the Cards.

She recommended that I get a book titled *Love Cards*, by Robert Camp, if I wanted to learn more. When I got the book and read what it said about a five of diamonds, it blew my mind. This was the missing piece of information that explained who I was. It described me almost perfectly. More than that, it helped me to understand myself from angles I had never perceived before.

As a five, it explained why I was so iconoclastic and introverted. As a diamond, it explained why I was very good at determining the quality and value of things. It opened a whole new world to me. I could now understand my strengths and weaknesses more clearly.

She told me that everyone matches their card. It's like your astrological Sun sign. You can't get away from it, because it's who you are.

The good thing about the Science of the Cards is that it is easy to learn. All you need is to read about two pages of information for your card, and then another page for each card type (heart, club, diamond, and spade). That's all you need. It's like your lifepath. You only need to read a few pages to learn quite a bit.

All of us are a combination of the four card types, but our dominant type almost always fits our card. To this day, I have never met anyone who did not match their type. Hearts are people you want to hug and have a love energy of some type. Clubs are smart and tend to be mostly in their head. Diamonds are creative in some way and know what has value. Spades are generally the most evolved and tend to be spiritually mature.

The other benefit from the Science of the Cards is how much more clearly I could see others by knowing their cards. If I know that your lifepath is a four, your card is a three of clubs, and your astrological sign is a Taurus, then that is a huge amount of information I know about you. I can get all of that information just from knowing your birthday. But I'm getting off the subject. That is just a side benefit. What we are after is to learn about ourselves so that we can communicate with our soul.

Michael Teachings

The Michael Teachings are a bit esoteric, but very powerful to understand. The original source of this information was channeled in the 1970s. I have written about the teachings in several of my books because I think they are important and valid. The teachings explain the reincarnation cycle. In my opinion, the two most important things to learn from the teachings are your role and your stage-level.

Everyone has a role, and some people have both a role and a sub-role. There are seven roles, and you should be able to guess your role. Here is the list, sorted by the fewest percentage of people with that role.

1. **King**: Leader (4%)
2. **Priest**: Spirituality/Inspiring (8%)
3. **Sage**: Performer/Communicator (10%)
4. **Scholar**: Collector of knowledge (14%)
5. **Warrior**: Achievement/Challenge (17%)

6. **Artisan**: Creative (22%)

7. **Server**: Server (25%)

As you can see, about 65% of the people fit into the last three categories. The top four categories are somewhat rare, with true leaders being the rarest role by far. You can guess your role by a process of elimination. Most people should be able to guess their role fairly accurately. Guessing your stage-level requires a bit more research.

I guessed that my role was a priest. The traits of a priest are explained in the teachings, as are the traits of all seven roles. When I was told in 1991 that my role was a priest with a sub-role of scholar, I wasn't sure about the sub-role. However, over the years, I have come to realize that I am a spiritual-scholar who collects and disseminates information for inspirational purposes.

Once you identify your role, it becomes a valuable piece of information about yourself. You may work in one profession, but your Michael Teaching's role could be completely different.

Once you know your role, the other piece of information that is useful is your stage-level. Everyone is at a particular level on their spiritual journey. You can think of it as a continuum that has a starting point that constantly increases (in fact, you cannot regress). Everyone begins their journey at the beginning of the continuum with very little to no understanding of the Creator. Then they slowly progress along the continuum, steadily increasing their knowing, leading to a comprehensive understanding of the Creator.

The Michael Teachings can help us to understand where we are on the continuum. If you study the teachings, there is enough information for you to make a good guess of where you are on the continuum. After I read a book on the Michael Teachings (there are several to choose from), I guessed that I was a mid-level old soul. Then I had a reading by a professional and found out that I am a 5th level old soul.

The continuum begins at the 1st level infant soul and rises to 7th level old soul. There are five stages and seven levels for each stage. There are thirty-five steps along the continuum. I am at the thirty-third step, and I am almost finished with this cycle. One cycle requires approximately 150 lifetimes. After I finish, I can begin again at the first step; or, if I am ready, I can choose to continue upward to become an ascended master.

Knowing where you are on the continuum is useful for achieving your life goals. It's another data point that is helpful in understanding who you are. Unfortunately, to find out where you are on the continuum, you need to read an entire book on the subject. Because, unless you read the material, you will not be able to guess where you are on the continuum or be able to confirm what someone else tells you in a reading.

I know the traits of a 5th level old soul from studying the Michael Teachings. After I was told that I was a 5th level old soul, I was able to confirm that it was a perfect fit. That was nearly thirty years ago. Since then, I have only had more confirmation that it is a perfect fit.

You may be thinking, why should I care about my role or where I am on the continuum? There are two reasons why I think it matters. First, your soul knows. Once you have this piece of information, it is another commonality that the soul can use to guide you. It allows you to get on the same page as the soul. Second, it helps you to understand your potential and your lessons. Each of the thirty-five steps consist of lessons that are described in the teachings.

As a fifth-level old soul, it is the last step before I pull away from society and devote myself to inner growth.

Most old souls that are 6th and 7th level generally keep to themselves in very quiet lifetimes. Knowing this is, perhaps, one of the reasons I am motivated to be a public writer. I'm sharing my knowledge because this is what fifth-level old souls do.

Part of me wants to have a quiet lifetime of introspection, but another part of me says that it is not time yet. I also realize that I chose a "1" lifepath, and my astrological sun is in my tenth house. Both of these placements are not for a quiet life of introspection. They are focused on being a self-starter and achieving something significant.

I have found that exposing myself to the Michael Teachings has given me more insight into people's behavior. For instance, you can often identify which roles your friends and colleagues are playing. Then you can guess if they are a young soul, mature soul, or old soul. This information can help in your pursuit of self-mastery. For instance, you will want to become better friends with the old souls that you know and those whose roles align with your own. Conversely, you will want to be wary of too much involvement with young and immature souls.

One thing that is crystal clear to me after studying the Michael Teachings is that everyone is at a certain level of spiritual maturity. Moreover, this level dictates the lessons that they will be learning in this lifetime. As someone who is pursuing self-mastery, I can understand the lessons being learned at each level by everyone. Then, I can adjust my life and personal relationships to adhere to this fact.

Everyone is already doing this to a high degree using their intuition. There are certain people you are attracted to and others that you are not. I have found that people who have a spade card are usually adept at reading others. As a diamond card and a Pisces, I'm not very good at reading others. For this reason, I use the Michael Teachings and other information to help me decipher other people's intentions. My older sister is a spade, and I can ask her about people when my intuition is hazy. Spades are great at recognizing the truth. They are often wise old souls.

This may sound odd, but one of the first things I do when someone new enters my life is to identify if they are a young, mature, or old soul. I often go further and attempt to identify which level they are on (one through seven). I'm pretty good at guessing after a few conversations.

You are going to learn a lot if you study the Michael Teachings. Each person has distinct characteristics that cannot be changed. We are what we are, and we are learning through a role. Trying to be something that you are not is not conducive to self-mastery. Knowing yourself and then attaining self-mastery is the key to both self-empowerment and spiritual awareness.

Mediums and Psychics

I have had a lot of readings in my life from mediums and psychics, although nearly all of them occurred in the 1990s when I was learning about myself. One thing you invariably learn from a reading is about yourself. Quite often, they will go on and on about our personality traits. When they start telling me about my personality traits, I usually have to stop them and say that I already know about myself and then guide them back to my questions.

If you are just beginning your spiritual journey, it is a good idea to have a few readings. If you select quality readers with good reputations, then you will end up learning quite a bit about yourself. If you have any strengths or weaknesses, or special abilities, these usually are mentioned by more than one reader. These will be confirmations that help you to learn about yourself, and perhaps what you are supposed to do in this lifetime.

One caveat to be aware of is that, if you have specific questions, you usually will not get an accurate answer. What I mean is that the answer provided usually is either not accurate or of little value. I have found that most of the valuable information that I have been given was not for the question I asked. It is better to ask broad questions and then see what you get. Keep your expectations low, kind of like when you buy a lottery ticket.

If you want the answer to a specific question, then do not expect to get an answer. The universe generally withholds information from us in order for us to learn our lessons. Also, because the success rate is so low for specific questions, do your own due diligence before choosing a reader. If you want to know something about your future, then you will need a talented reader, and even then, the information may not be forthcoming.

E-Colors

There are quite a few personality tests that you can take. One that I like is E-Colors. It is free and only takes about 15 minutes to answer 35 questions. It's been around for many years and has been used by thousands of people. It works very well at identifying personality types.

At one company where I worked, everyone had to take the survey. What was interesting is that most of the managers had a dominant color of red (The Doer), and most of the people in the IT department had a dominant color of green (The Thinker).

What is useful with E-Colors is not necessarily your strongest traits, because most of these will be known to you. What is useful are the negative aspects of your strongest traits. Those are the traits that you need to control, or else they can undermine your goals and relationships. These are the traits that prevent you from self-mastery.

The other thing that is useful is reading the positive and negative traits for each of the four color personalities (red, green, blue, and yellow). These descriptions are like getting a course in psychology. What's interesting is that everyone has a dominant color, and that color plays a huge role in their personality. Moreover, each color has both positive traits and negative traits.

Once you learn the traits for each color, you will have insight into the behavior of others. It is usually pretty easy to guess other people's dominant color, and if you know that someone has a dominant color, then you know quite a bit about that person. Why? Because each of the four colors has a known list of positive and negative traits.

All of the various ways that we can use to learn about ourselves gives us insight into others. For instance, I know some of the traits of each sign and some of the traits of each color. If I know that someone is a particular sign and a particular color, that knowledge is going to help me make my day go more harmoniously. Moreover, it is going to help me with self-mastery. It is much more difficult to push my buttons when I know what type of behavior can result from those traits.

As the saying goes, knowledge is power. And whereas the truth might not set you free, the more truth you have is a good thing. If you want to attain self-mastery, then you want to know as much truth about yourself and others as possible.

The Ego

The next chapter is Finding Your Soul. In that chapter, I will show you how to find your soul by marginalizing your ego. The process of marginalizing your ego will expose it in a way that will help you to learn more about yourself. The ego is secretive and tries to hide. The ego does not want you to expose it because that lessens its control, which it is determined to maintain. Self-mastery is attained by disarming the ego and placing your soul in charge.

Perhaps the most important thing you can do to attain self-mastery is to understand how the ego controls you, and then take the required steps to remove its control. This requires a process, which I have outlined in the next chapter.

Combining Everything

Once you have collected all of the information that I have suggested in this chapter, you will have a picture of who you are. The Creator is not hiding this information. It is there for everyone to find. All you need is the desire and intent to find it.

Once you have gathered this information, it has to be assimilated. This requires some time. I would say it will take at least a year and, perhaps, several years to assimilate. You will need to process this information in your mind and come to the realization of what it means. After all, it is a lot of information to absorb.

Over time, you will start to see how your astrology, numerology, card, role, stage-level, E-Colors, ego, mission, and soul lessons all intertwine to create you. Both your positive and negative traits will become consciously known to you, along with the soul lessons you are trying to accomplish. Also, there is a chance you will recognize an overall mission that you are trying to achieve.

After going through this process of self-discovery, I can understand why so few go down this path. Why? Because it inevitably becomes a very humbling experience. Most people prefer to focus only on their positive traits and pretend that they don't have any negative traits. That's not possible once you begin self-discovery. Also, it can be a bit depressing discovering what you are not. For instance, you will learn all of the positive traits that other people possess that you do not. That can be humbling.

CHAPTER SIXTEEN

Finding Your Soul

I wrote an entire book on how to find your soul. In this chapter, I will give you an overview. This is all new information that is not included in that book.

I remember once, I was at a new age expo, and someone came up to my booth, which had a poster of my book. He laughed and said, "Why do I need to find my soul? Where did it go?" He was making a joke, but, whereas most people assume they have a soul that is always with them, very few attempt to communicate with it directly. I told him that it really wasn't about finding his soul, but learning how to communicate with it. I could have called the book, "Communicating with Your Soul," but that doesn't have the same ring to it.

Finding your soul is much easier for women because they are more connected to their heart-center. The Creator made women this way so that it would ensure the survival of human beings. This allows women to feel and hear their soul in a more dynamic way than men. They can follow guidance from their soul much easier than men.

I don't think it is an accident that Mary Magdalene was referred to in the Gnostic gospels as the Apostle of the Apostles, and was the most spiritually aware of all the apostles. In the Gnostic gospels that were discovered in the eighteenth century, Jesus says, "Mary, thou blessed one, whom I will perfect in all mysteries … whose heart is raised to the kingdom of heaven more than all thy brethren." Why was Mary the most spiritually aware? Likely, because she was a woman, which gave her a more open connection to her soul. This is also why so many women were murdered in Europe, accused of being witches.

Fortunately, this gateway to our soul has recently been opening up for men as well. This began in the late nineteenth century and has been steadily increasing in strength. The energy frequency of the planet is currently changing, making it more conducive for anyone to open up the gateway to their soul. If you want to read more about this energy shift, there is a plethora of information available on the Internet.

* * * * *

We each have two voices in our head, and knowing which is which, is not always easy. In fact, for most people, they can't tell the difference. One voice is your ego, and the other is your soul. Actually, one is the gateway to the other side of the veil. This gateway can bring in information from a variety of sources, such as your higher self, angels, spirit guides, and discarnate beings.

We are constantly given guidance from the other side. This guidance is usually so subtle that we don't even recognize it. We think it is the same voice that we always hear, but it is not. The soul communicates with us in a variety of ways, the most powerful of which is feeling. These are feelings that we translate into words. Often, these words are silent and subtle. So, ultimately, finding the soul is about hearing the soul, even if, sometimes, these words appear to be silent.

The voices that we hear and the words that we feel come from either the ego or the soul. Knowing the difference is not easy. In fact, it is often impossible. The primary difference between these two sources is that one (the ego) wants to control you, and the other (the soul) wants to help you. Because the ego is only concerned with its survival – which is accomplished through controlling us – it needs to be marginalized, which I'm going to show you how to do.

There is a lot of complexity involved in finding your soul. In fact, it requires a lot of effort on your part. To find your soul, you have to speak the same language as the soul. You have to be on the same wavelength. This requires intent and effort.

The soul exists in a place of purity and innocence. If there is such a thing as perfect virtue, then that is where the soul resides. That is the energy that you need to connect with and listen to. As you can imagine, that is not anything remotely similar to the ego. This is the first clue on recognizing the difference between these two voices.

To find the soul, you have to know what to listen for, but you also have to be prepared to listen. This can't be done carelessly or with nonchalance. It has to be proactive and with intent.

This took me several years to understand, and now I am prepared to give you instructions on how to do it. I have become awestruck at the dichotomy of how difficult it is versus how simple it is – if you know how. After you read this chapter, you will know how. So, pay attention.

The starting point is putting yourself in a position to be able to hear the soul and know that it is the soul that is communicating with you. To achieve this, you have to marginalize the ego and become aligned with the soul.

I'm going to warn you right now that the ego is very powerful and will do everything it can to prevent you from marginalizing it. The ego only has one mission, and that is to control you. You can think of the ego as a powerful artificial intelligence that is conscious and does not want you to turn it off.

We have two challenges that we have to overcome to find our soul. The first is that we have to get the ego out of the way, and the second is that we have to be able to communicate with our soul. Thankfully, both challenges can be addressed at the same time.

The only way to marginalize the ego is to become virtuous. Virtue is the language of the soul. By becoming virtuous, you align with the soul to combat the ego. Moreover, by being virtuous, you attract the soul because that is where it abides.

Okay, here is what you have to do. It won't be easy, but it is possible, and the benefits are infinite if you succeed. Every morning when you wake up, you have to align yourself with your soul. You have to create a routine that places you with the intent to live a virtuous day. Here is my current routine (my routine has changed many times).

1. Shower and shave.
2. Stretch for five minutes (stretching is very beneficial once you turn 50).
3. Make breakfast.
4. Say the Lord's Prayer aloud, with reverence.
5. Say my hand prayer aloud.
6. Eat breakfast.
7. Take supplements.
8. Clean my dishes.
9. Begin my day.

My hand prayer has changed many times, but the theme and intent are still the same, which is to live with virtue that day. Each digit on my hands represents something I am going to say aloud. I used to wiggle my thumbs and fingers, but now I just say the number.

Here is my current hand prayer:

Left thumb. "One: Respect the soul. Keep it clear, keep it clean, keep it healthy." This is in regard to my aura and my soul energy field.

Left index finger. "Two: Have faith. Respect the perfection. Trust the plan. Remain claim." This is in regard to trusting God and my life's plan, which only God knows.

Left middle finger. "Three: Respect others. Be nice, be friendly, gentle, caring, compassionate, concerned." This is in regard to how I will treat others on that day.

Left ring finger. "Four: Know the mission. Serve, give, help to humanity." This is in regard to my blueprint, which is to be a lightworker and help humanity advance to a new civilization.

Left pinky finger. "Five: Be focused, committed, and mindful of that objective." This is in regard to reinforcing my focus on my life lesson.

Right thumb. "Six: Pride. Puffiness, arrogance, lack of gratitude. Be the best version of Don." This is in regard to combating the ego.

Right index finger. "Seven: Ego. Hedonism. Lust, appetites, addictions. Don't be dope (dopamine rush), don't be a dorf (endorphin rush). Don't let the little man (your ego) trick you." This is in regard to combating the ego from enticing you with temptation.

Right middle finger. "Eight: Stay present. Stay open. Be humble. You're not doing this on your own." This is in regard to connecting to your higher self and keeping that channel open.

Right ring finger. "Nine: It's not about me. It's about we." This is in regard to recognizing that everyone and everything is connected.

Right pinky finger. "Ten: Gratitude is my attitude. Food on the table, roof over my head, money in the bank, family and friends, healthy body, spirit guides, opportunity." This is in regard to acknowledging what the Creator has given me."

I finish by saying, "Namaste." This is in regard to acknowledging my spirit guides who are with me, and to complete the prayer. Then it's time to eat my breakfast, which is always sitting in front of me when I begin the prayer.

The hand prayer only takes about two minutes to complete and sets the tone for the day. As I progress through the day, I constantly remind myself that I am abiding by my commitment to that morning prayer. I try to remain humble and gracious to those with whom I interact. I try to remain virtuous at all times.

During the day, I reflect if I am in accordance with the hand prayer and my daily intent to be virtuous. There are days when I recognize that I have failed, which is a failure at self-mastery. I make a conscious effort to begin again the next day with my mission to succeed at self-mastery.

Now, you may think that this is overkill and that I should just go live my life. However, I have found that this is the only way to connect with the soul on a deep level, while at the same time disconnecting from the ego, which is my objective. For this same outcome, you have to do it day after day, and it takes practice.

When I started out marginalizing my ego, each morning I had to write down where I had stumbled the previous day. The stumbles were clear to me, as the ego made its presence known and wanted to be in control. Slowly, I had to consciously become aware of my ego's shenanigans. God purposely tests us, and the ego is how these tests are performed. You will inevitably find out where the ego is hiding because your unvirtuous behavior will surface. That is, unless you are a saint.

Once you begin living a virtuous life, the soul will appear. I would be very surprised if it does not. It will appear because it wants to guide you if you are in alignment. The guidance will be subtle, but you will begin to feel it. The key will be *allowing* it to lead. You do this by feeling your way through life. This is why women have an advantage in this area. They are naturally intuitive and are better at feeling their emotions and becoming heart-led.

Once you get the ego out of the way, the soul is ready to lead. All you need to do is keep a quiet mind and allow your emotions to arise on their own. The ego will push back at this new-found way of living. The ego will try to chatter in your head and give you direction, but you must learn how to keep it quiet (one way to do this is through meditation).

What is magical is that the soul will come to your rescue in your battle with the ego. The soul will help, and all you need to do is ask it each and every morning. Your morning hand prayer to live a virtuous day is exactly what the soul wants you to do. That is how you get in alignment with the soul. Once you find areas where the ego is intruding on your virtue, ask the soul for help in these areas.

Unfortunately, your ego will use your bad habits to stay in control. The soul will help you to remove these bad habits, but the ego will have its say. For this reason, you will need to spend a lot of time removing bad habits. This will not be easy. I can understand why people become monks when they decide to go on a spiritual journey, because it can feel like it requires all of your time and attention to be virtuous.

Once you begin living a virtuous life, it is inevitable that you will find areas of your life that need work. Don't try to fix everything all at once. Instead, fix one thing at a time. Let your feelings tell you what needs to be worked on. In the new age movement, some people call this clearing. You have to clear out all of your emotional baggage and become clear and clean. Often, bad habits are directly related to this baggage. It's like junk in your garage that needs to be tossed out.

If you try to go down this path of becoming virtuous, it will only be a matter of time before you and your soul are on the same wavelength. For many of you, your spirit guides or higher self might begin talking to you. For others, you will get strong feelings on how to make better choices. If you don't feel any spiritual guidance, I would be surprised.

Ironically, when you stop directing your life through your ego, you won't let anyone else direct it, either. What happens is that, once you begin to allow your soul to guide you, no one else will be able to. You will become a very stubborn person who demands inner guidance. You will learn that only you know what's good for you. You will be inner-directed. Once you get to this place, it will feel like home. This is the *way*, and you will know it.

Most of the people around you who are ego-directed will not like the new you. This is ironic since it is an improved version of yourself. You will become something that they do not understand, and people reject what they fear. So, if you experience some rejection, that is to be expected. People will misinterpret your inner guidance for narcissism and selfishness.

The key to knowing that you have found your soul is the loss of fear, especially the fear of death. The reason for this is that you will come to understand that the soul is the real you and that the soul is eternal. You may have some fear of leaving this lifetime early because of FOMO (fear of missing out), but the fear of death should subside dramatically.

This lifetime will begin to feel like a transitory thing, much like taking a vacation or attending an event. Once you become aware that you are an eternal being, your frame of reference begins to change. You start to see this lifetime from a different perspective. For instance, I now think of this lifetime as a blip of experience in the overall life of my soul. That's all it is, a blip! That is completely different from my perspective before I began my spiritual journey.

I am a fifth-level old soul priest, so it was inevitable that I found my soul in this lifetime. What surprised me was the tenacity and strength of the ego. I couldn't believe how much effort was required to marginalize the ego. However, if I wanted my soul to be in charge, then I had to find a way to marginalize the ego. I found that living a virtuous life was the only way it could be marginalized.

The key to finding your soul – and allowing your soul to lead you – is opening your heart and becoming humble and grateful. If you want to be awakened, then try to understand that previous sentence. Understanding that sentence is only possible if you recognize and become aware of what your soul really is – a piece of God.

Ironically, most religions do not teach that there is a path to enlightenment that can be found within. I think the reason why is because, until this generation, it was a very difficult path for most people. It was really only a path for old souls to tread. However, the energy vibration on the planet has changed and made this path more accessible to everyone.

Being a fifth-level old soul priest-scholar, who better to tell the world how to find their soul? I'm not that shocked that these words spill out of me, even though the vast majority of people have no idea what I am writing about. Only about five percent (in 2023) of the global population *knows* that God exists. Most people live on faith that God exists. However, if you follow the guidance that I have given in this chapter, you will likely find both your soul and God at the same time. You will join the legions who are awakening.

Virtues / Truth Bombs / Affirmations

Here is a list of virtues. These should be our goal.

Honesty/Trustworthy

Humble/Humility

Gratitude/Grateful

Good/Honorable

Purity/Innocence

Integrity/Honor

Decency/Propriety

Tolerance/Unconditional Love

Benevolence/Fairness

Ethical/Blameless

Charity/Giving

Temperance/Patience

Ascetic/Pious

Service/Nurture

Respect/Courtesy

Courage/Passion

Here is a list of truth bombs/affirmations. I like to write these on the back of business cards and read them at stop signs when I'm driving around town.

We are God, and so is everyone and everything else.

Everyone's life is perfect.

Everyone creates their own reality by their beliefs.

There are no accidents.

Life is an illusion.

Reincarnation is a reality.

Spirituality is a personal matter.

You are God.

You have lived many lives, each bringing you closer to enlightenment.

You carefully planned this life before you were born.

You are not alone in carrying out your plan.

You will not experience anything you do not want to experience.

Your life is perfect.

Everything is perfect.

Everything happens for a reason.

Nothing new can ever happen – everything happening has already happened.

Do not take life too seriously.

Walk with a light step and an easy smile.

Be kind and generous.

Love everyone.

Relish each day.

Be happy.

Trust the Universe to only give you what you need.

Have a plan.

Find something to do that you enjoy.

Higher spiritual life is service to humanity.

Matthew 22:37 Love God with all your heart, all your soul, all your mind.

Love your neighbor as yourself.

The purpose of one's life is to be a conscious instrument of the divine presence.

Be the best version of you.

Be an example: live with gratitude, virtue, and integrity. Shine your light.

The spirit is willing, but the flesh is weak.

Maintain a love frequency: remain neutral, and accept all that happens with equanimity.

Be grateful for all that happens.

Embrace uncertainty: stay calm and stay present with a feeling of inner peace.

Nothing works for those who don't do the work.

The ego prefers entertainment, hedonism, constant pleasure, and selfish me-focus.

The path to success: focus (on what is necessary), intent (achieve you soul's objective), and discipline (daily habits).

The higher you align, the more you shine.

Trust the perfection, trust the plan.

Marginalize the ego.

Mindset: an objective, goals, intent, daily habits, accumulate knowledge.

Heartset: improve your relationships.

Healthset: eat right, exercise, take supplements, rest

Soulset: marginalize the ego, be a conscious instrument of the divine presence, stay connected to the heart.

The 4 Nobel Truths:

1. Suffering is inevitable without enlightenment.

2. The cause of suffering is craving.

3. The cessation of suffering comes from right thinking.

4. Right thinking comes from a spiritual path.

You attract events in your life via your beliefs and intent (stay positive, or else you will attract negative events).

Belief/intent creates our reality.

Our soul vibration/tone creates our reality.

Joy attracts joy, light attracts light, expect trouble and receive trouble, expect love and receive love.

Be positive and attract positive outcomes, expect a good outcome to attract one.

Only make choices for your highest good.

Be the peace you want to see.

Don't be a slave to your appetites, addictions.

Don't make low consciousness decisions.

Self love, self respect is the key to it all. This is ultimately what creates outcomes.

True happiness comes from accepting each moment and appreciating each moment. This is a place of neutrality, which is unconditional love.

Consciousness is separate from the brain. This is why people who have NDEs feel the same when they pop out of their bodies.

The soul has infinite potential and is in continuous expansion. Awareness of this should create peace of mind.

The soul is striving to remember who and what it is: a piece of the creator.

A utopian society: this is what we are creating, based on love.

To overcome societal conflict, be yourself, be an example, and be a frequency of love.

Each soul must find the truth on their own.

Gratitude should lead to virtue and integrity, or else gratitude is false.

If you are not fixing the problem, you are part of the problem (darkness).

The only blasphemy is the denial of the divine.

Separation is a lie, a false belief.

We are not separate from the Creator (God).

We are not separate from anyone or anything.

All is divine, all is connected.

Desire-lessness and disinterest of temptation is the liberator.

People think they are separate from source, which is a lie.

What is true is always true.

Fear and the truth cannot coexist.

I AM / God Is.

All problems are manifested from the denial of the divine.

Stay positive, don't let fear in.

Telepathy will soon become common.

Deep contentment with our true self and reality is possible.

In the future, we stop eating animals because it emphasizes duality (we think we are separate from them, but we are not).

Co-resonance: Judge darkness, and you attract it to you. Bless it and it blesses you back

Discernment, discretion, and wisdom come from the soul and not from learning knowledge.

To dam another is to dam yourself. To bless another is to bless yourself.

Life events only have two outcomes: an opportunity (something to learn) or a blessing (something learned).

Life is a blessing. Live that way. Live with gratitude.

Expect good things. Create good things.

The divine only knows wellness, success, joy, aliveness, and unlimitedness. Remain positive in this energy to be in alignment with the divine.

You pull yourself down with your thoughts and beliefs.

I am loved. I am supported. I AM.

As you become more aware, seeking is replaced by being.

Vibrate in success and joy. You are here. You made it. You created this lifetime.

Accept all that happens in the present moment with constant gratitude and an ongoing state of neutrality. This is the frequency of unconditional love.

Make the present moment your friend and not your enemy.

The more you love yourself, the more it will be reflected back to you.

To judge another is confirm your own place there.

To forgive another is to set yourself free.

How to live: Desire > Passion > Creation. Follow your heart. It is true.

What if something bad happens? What if something good happens? Both are beliefs. You can believe either. Fear is an idea/belief.

Embrace uncertainty. Live without fear. Stay positive. Stay present.

Fear is not real. Fear is an idea. Fear is the denial of the divine.

Fear is not wise. Fear's goal is to exist.

Where does our knowing of right and wrong come from? Is it taught? No. We bring it with us. Our consciousness is intelligent.

When people have NDEs they are shocked that they are intelligent without a brain. Our consciousness is our soul.

Suggested Reading

The Kingdome, Paul Selig (The Guides)

Anna, Grandmother of Jesus, Claire Heartsong (Anna)

The Serpent of Light, Druvalo Melchizedek

Think on These Things, J. Krishnamurti

Seat of the Soul, Gary Zukav

A New Earth, Eckhart Tolle

The Disappearance of the Universe, Gary Renard (Ascended Masters)

Journey of Souls, Michael Newton

The New Revelations, Neale Donald Walsch (God)

The P'taah Tapes, Jani King (P'taah)

Power Versus Force, David Hawkins

The Messengers, G.W. Hardin

Holy Blood Holy Grail, Michael Baigent

The Woman with the Alabaster Jar, Margaret Starbird

The Da Vinci Code, Dan Brown

Messages From Michael, Chelsea Quinn Yarbro (Michael)

Notes from the Cosmos, Gordon-Michael Scallion

The Key, Whitley Strieber

Do not Think Like a Human, **Lee Carroll (Kryon)**

Seth Speaks, **Jane Roberts (Seth)**

Talking to Heaven, **James Van Praagh**

Planetary Brother, **Mary Margaret Moore (Bartholomew)**

Mutant Messages Down Under, **Marlo Morgan**

Star Signs, **Linda Goodman**

The Edgar Cayce Companion, **B. Ernest Frejer**

The Indigo Children, **Jan Tober and Lee Carroll**

Emissary of Light, **James Twyman**

Old Souls, **Tom Shroder**

Talking to Extraterrestrials, **Lisette Larkins**

Where Two Worlds Touch, **Gloria Karpinski**

Blue Print for Change, **Darryl Anka (Bashar)**

Emmanual's Book, **unknown channel (Emmanual)**

The Sacred Journey, **Jach Pursel (Lazaris)**

God I Am, **Peter Erbe**

The Starseed Transmissions **Ken Carey (Raphael)**

Grist for the Mill, **Ram Dass**

Bringers of the Dawn, **Barbara Marciniak (The Pleiadians)**

Earthly Purpose, **Dick Sutphen**

Many Lives Many Masters, **Dr. Brian Weiss**

Way of the Peaceful Warrior, **Dan Millman**

Conversations With Nostradamus, **Dolores Cannon (Nostradamus)**

The Fatima Prophecy, **Ray Stanford**

Ramtha, **J.Z. Knight (Ramtha)**

Aliens Among Us, **Ruth Montgomery**

Abraham Speaks, **Ester Hicks (Abraham)**

Mass Dreams of the Future, **Chet Snow**

Mary's Message to the World, **Annie Kirkwood (Mother Mary)**

Man's Eternal Quest, **Paramahansa Yogananda**

We the Arcturians, **Norma Milanovich**

The Ringing Cedars Series, **Vladimire Megre**

Love Cards, **Robert Camp**

Glynis Has Your Number, **Robert Camp**

Card of Destiny, **Sharon Jeffers**

The Life You Were Born to Live, **Dan Millman**

Earth, the Cosmos, and You, **Orpheus Phylos and Virgina Essene (Archangel Michael)**

YouTube Channel for Channeler Interviews: @ **NextLevelSoul**

YouTube Channel for NDE Interviews: @ **LoveCoverdLifePodcast**

GoFundMe

If you enjoyed the book and would like the opportunity to help fund marketing so that more people are exposed to these ideas, I created a GoFundMe page.

Every dollar donated will be spent on advertising the book. You can lend a hand in spreading this information.

Go to GoFundMe.com and search for:

Your Soul Explained

You will see the book cover in the search results.

If you have any questions, my contact information is on my website: www.dondurrett.com